He's the
Weird Teacher

and other things students whisper about me

by Doug Robertson

ISBN-13: 978-1492193838
ISBN-10: 1492193836

More info:
Website: http://hestheweirdteacher.blogspot.com/

Book design: Y42K Book Production Services
http://www.y42k.com/bookproduction.html

For:
Bethany and Matt
~ for teaching me to be a better teacher

&

Angela and Roland
~ for teaching me to be a better human

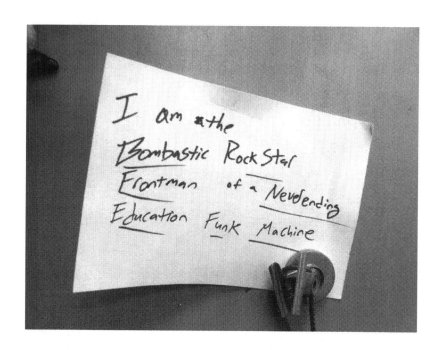

Table of Contents

Forward 1

Chapter 1: Rockstar 3

Chapter 2: Personal Responsibility 7

Chapter 3: Teaching Is Performance Art 15

Chapter 4: Polar Express 25

Chapter 5: Distractions 31

Chapter 6: Student Teachers 41

Chapter 7: Philosophy on Discipline 51

Chapter 8: When the Students Are Hard You're Doing Your Job 61

Chapter 9: Dressing Up 67

Chapter 10: How You Talk When You Talk About Your Students 73

Chapter 11: The Trunchbull and *Deep Breath* Parents .. 79

Chapter 12: Bodily Functions 89

Chapter 13: Indoor Recess is Evil 95

Chapter 14: The "E" Word 103

Chapter 15: Bullying 109

Chapter 16: Letters To Prison 117

Chapter 17: Spelling Tests 123

Chapter 18. My First Staff Meeting 129

Chapter 19: What I Want Out of an Administrator 133

Chapter 20: Learn From Fear/Inspire With Love 139

Chapter 21: Getting a Tie and Losing My Music 147

Chapter 22: Strange Things I Do In My Classroom (OR Things I Think I Might Have Stolen)................................ 153

Chapter 23: Special Guests................................ 163

Chapter 24: Peanut Butter and Jelly Sandwiches............ 171

Chapter 25: Tetherball 177

Chapter 26: Sympathy for the Weird Kid 185

Chapter 27: Messing with Kindergarteners.................... 193

Chapter 28: Suck It! 201

Chapter 29: There Are No Rules and Everyone Is Faking It 207

Chapter 30: Reading Above Their Level......................... 215

Chapter 31: Substitutes.. 223

Chapter 32: Dinosaurs and Fields of Study 231

Chapter 33: Safe Schools....................................... 235

Chapter 34: The System.. 239

Chapter 35: Hello, Goodbye and Thank You 253

Thank You 257

About the Author 259

Forward

As Mr. Robertson wrote, "Every class has at least one. The kid that is just a little bit more unique than everyone else." I am that weird girl mentioned in Chapter 26. Even before finding out through shrubbery that we were both weird, I knew Mr. Robertson was an awesome teacher. Why? Because he's awesome. His classroom was fun and a good learning environment. He expects the best in his class and he gets it. After reading this book I discovered things that even I, as a past student, didn't know. But I can say that I recognized most of what he wrote and know it's true. You should read this book for many reasons, such as learning how a classroom can be exciting, and discovering ways to create a fun place for children/students/munchkins to learn. But *He's the Weird Teacher* is not just about cramming information about teaching into your head; it also contains some humor. It is about the philosophy of teaching and stuff like that.

-- Katja La Flamme, age 11

Doug Robertson takes all the creative energy and zany antics he uses to inspire the students in his classroom and has channeled it into a fun to read, irreverent, but deeply meaningful guide to teaching.

-- Her mom (wannabe roadie in the education funk machine)

1

Doug Robertson

Chapter 1: Rockstar

I keep a very basic version of my teaching philosophy written on a notecard and stuck to the filing cabinet next to my desk, where it is easy to read whenever I need to. It's not fancy, because I'm not really a fancy sign kind of teacher. In fact, when I thought of it I quickly grabbed a Sharpie (a teacher's best friend) and scribbled it down. That's the draft I stuck up. Yes, Mr. Robertson has a first draft on display in his classroom. Oh, what would the students think?

It's not *really* on display though. I would bet none of my students know this notecard exists. My student teachers probably do, they often sit at my desk to work. An observant substitute would notice it. The reason my Sharpie notecard teaching philosophy isn't on display for all to see is because it is kind of silly. Well, you might think it is silly. I think it pretty perfectly sums up what I'm trying to get across when I'm teaching. I've never mentioned it to anyone before. Not even my student teachers, and I talk to them about everything that barely even falls near the periphery of education. But I like you, dear reader. Simply by holding this you've shown impeccable taste. If you lean in close I will tell you my simple, distilled teaching philosophy. The thing I cling to when I'm worn out, tired, grumpy, or waiting desperately for the coffee to kick in. Ready?

I am the Bombastic Rockstar Frontman of a Never-Ending Education Funk Machine.

I should explain.

I listen to a lot of music. My favorite bands have always been the ones with the true Rockstar Frontman. Think Steven Tyler, but without the substance abuse and prior to becoming a walking self-parody. So, think Steven Tyler circa *Permanent*

Vacation - Nine Lives. If you saw Tyler on stage in that period of Aerosmith's life you know what I'm talking about. Complete control of the audience, boundless energy, amazing talent. Think Henry Rollins. Powerful, explosive, aggressive, full tilt boogie from the first note to the final cymbal crash. You leave the show knowing the music was all he cared about. Bombastic and straight ahead. That's what I'm going for.

Teaching, like music, is a performance art. Good performers are aware of and engaged with the audience. They draw the audience in and make them want to participate. Make them want to be a part of the show. Infect them with the energy. Is the energy always there? No. Bands have off nights. The key is that the audience never knows if you're off or not. That's professional. That's part of being a Rockstar Frontman.

Teaching is experimental theater. I don't know if a lot of the things I try in front of my class are going to land. Some of them will fail. Some will fail hard. But that is always better than teaching the same thing in the same way for years on end. Teaching is a never-ending quest for perfection. I try different things all the time. If I'm bored then I know the students are bored. I know teachers who have taught the same grade at the same school in the same classroom for years and years. One opinion on that would be, "Well, then they must be very good at what they do." And that's true. Repetition breeds familiarity. Malcolm Gladwell, in his amazing book *Outliers*, said that it takes 10,000 hours of doing something before you can be truly great at it. There is a line though, especially in something like teaching, where you become too set in your ways. Teachers become part of their classrooms and even teachers with the best of intentions stagnate. "Because this is how we've always done it," is a common refrain when teachers push back against change. It is also just about the worst reason for doing anything I can think of. It's not that these are bad teachers, it's just that these are teachers who have stopped growing and experimenting. Those ideas and more will be explored throughout the pages of this book.

As a bombastic rock star frontman of a never-ending education funk machine I embody intensity in ten cities. I have to bring it every day because my audience expects nothing less than my best. I should be on my game even when I feel off because rock stars don't miss a gig. The class isn't just the audience, though. Not in my room, not with how I view learning. The class is my band and I am their band leader. I set the tone, I tell them when to bring it up and I tell them when to break it down. I wave the stick and they bang the drum. Together we make music. The education funk machine is all about finding that deep groove and settling in until something moves you out of it. A new kid, a different set of standards, a change in the tests, boredom, the need for new.

A machine never stops, it doesn't rest. I listen for creaks and squeaks and rattling and strains. I care for the machine, constantly oiling, constantly improving, constantly updating. An education machine can crank away all day, a Terminator-like AI, learning the best way to teach you. I have detailed files to make me a more effective information imparting organism.

Knowing that I'm forever striving to be a bombastic rock star frontman of a never-ending education funk machine keeps me positive in the classroom. Funk is not angry. Funk doesn't shout at you when you mess up. Funk is love. Teaching is love.

Doug Robertson

Chapter 2: Personal Responsibility

Fair warning- this is a Soapbox Chapter. There may be proselytizing.

I take teaching very personally. Everything about it. I believe down to my toes that the things that happen in my classroom reflect me as a teacher more than they reflect anything else. In my room I am the guide, the leader, the Grand High Emperor of All and Beyond, and what happens to my students when they are under my care rests solely with me. Every grade, every project, every action outside my classroom while they're in school between those bells starts and ends with me.

Why? Because I'm the adult. I'm the Teacher.

I expect my students to take personal responsibility for themselves in school. I think all teachers do. That's Rule #1 in most classes and the first place you go to as a teacher when you're having a Disciplinary Talk. "And who decided to do *x*, *y*, *z*? Why was it your choice?" Sometimes we go with the cliched, "If all your friends decided to jump off the building would you?" but I think that's asking for a smart-aleck response. Lincoln said never ask a question you don't want an answer to. The other option, "Was someone holding a gun to your head?" gets less metaphorical and more frightening every week so let's not go there anymore, huh? I don't know if all teachers model the behavior they say they expect from their students at school, but I do. I try not to expect my students to do anything that I don't do.

It is easy for teachers to not take full and total responsibility for the learning that happens in their classroom. It might even be healthier not to. I know I am not the only factor in a child's life. I get them for six hours a day. I should be taking into account their parents, their home life, their economic situation, and their background when I think about their performance. But I don't. I don't because I don't think responsibility is normally seen as a two-way street. When a child does well you're a great teacher. When a child struggles his parents aren't helping enough at home. You can't have it both ways. Either you, the teacher, are the final word or you aren't.

Not to say parents aren't important. Not in the least. Parents are incredibly important to a child's development and education. Good parents can make a world of difference and bad parents can put a child at a severe disadvantage. But they are not the be all and end all. I've had parents that make me think of The Simpsons episode when we learn about Ned Flanders's childhood. His parents are sitting in a child psychiatrist's office while little Ned tears the place up and the father says, "You've gotta help us, doc. We've tried nothing and we're all out of ideas!" I've had good kids from bad homes and troublemakers with the best parents you can think of.

More to the point, the parents aren't the ones in my classroom. I'm not teaching them. That's not my job.

I'll reach out. I send notes home all the time. I have meetings. Well, I call meetings and sometimes someone shows up. I'm all about home communication. I started a homework blog so that anyone can see exactly what the homework is every day. I post detailed descriptions of the projects we are working on. I have due dates and important dates highlighted at the top of the page. At the start of the year I send home a note with the web address so every parent can find the page and I bring it up again during Parent/Teacher Conferences once I realize that no one kept/read that paper. I've optimized the website so it even looks sharp on a smart phone. I do this so I know there is absolutely no reason someone shouldn't know what the homework is. I'm positive I've done everything I can to inform the parents and the students what is expected of them each day. I don't even write the blog after the first week of school. It's a job I give to my class secretary so the students have a more personal investment in it.

My homework blog gets maybe two hits a day.

That bums me out. If, when my son gets to school-age, his teacher has a website that gets updates daily with assignments and information I'll be checking that thing every day. I'll be leaving comments on posts. It'll be bookmark numero uno on my web browser. Not because I won't trust my son, but because my son will be a child and it's my job as the parent to keep him on task. That means double checking his work even when I know he's not lying. That's not distrust; that's covering my bases. His teacher had better have a website too. He won't be in kindergarten until 2018. That's the future! I'll be dropping him off in my flying car by then.

This sense of deep personal responsibility comes from my parents, but it also comes from lifeguarding, the best job I ever had. I worked at a pool every summer for years in the City of Palmdale. When I was a lifeguard I worked with an old timer named Brian Yepp. Brian was Yoda. He had been guarding since the pools were dirt holes in the desert filled with rainwater. Brian had guarding down to a science, and he painstakingly trained us in his image. He used to question us all the time, not just on skills but on our motivations and our choices in and around the pool. He was Yoda and we all saw him that way. I, at least, bought in completely. He had that kind of personality where you wanted to prove to him you could do it, and you wanted him to be proud of you. If I practiced a skill in front of Brian and got a nod that made my day. During my rookie training I was a better swimmer than most other guards and was doing well enough in the swim workouts, finishing before most everyone else and getting plenty of rest. He knew I wasn't swimming as hard as I could. I was brought into the office and he told me I wasn't working hard enough in no uncertain terms. Beating everyone else wasn't the goal. Bettering myself was.

I worked harder.

I've stolen a lot from Brian. He was a lawyer and used lawyer tricks on us. He used to fix us in a stare and ask about a questionable choice we may have made. He'd ask the question, and then always follow it up with this statement, "Remember, I don't ask questions unless I know the answer first." That was probably a lie 50% of the time. He might not know the answer. But why take that chance? He certainly *looked* like he knew the answer. I pull that on my kids all the time. I dare you to lie to me, because I know what the answer really is and I'll catch you.

Brian knew that we were only as strong as our weakest link. At the pool you do most saves alone, but the important ones take a team. Spinals, when a victim has injured their neck or back, ideally take four guards to do. A spinal save has lots of moving parts, from immobilizing the head and neck, not easy in the water, to preparing the spine board, to getting the victim out of the pool. All of this has to be done smoothly and calmly because if you disturb the water too much the victim may float out of alignment and if there is swelling in the spinal column that's bad news. Four guards working together. Everyone had to know every step of the dance, your moves and your partner's. You took it personally, because if you didn't you might be the reason someone ends up in a wheelchair. Brian drilled that into our heads. He demanded excellence. "This ain't McDonalds," he'd say. "You mess up working at McDonalds, someone gets a burnt burger. You mess up here, someone could die."

My classroom is not life and death. Just life, the future lives of the children in my care.

Education is a building and you need every floor to be complete before you start the next. The child needs a strong foundation from home and kindergarten. First grade takes that foundation and builds the support structure, second adds, and so on. Any weakness at any point means two things. One- the next teacher has to go back and shore up that weakness. Two- that shoring-up holds the child back from getting what they need in that grade level. I tease the kindergarten teachers sometimes because that's where it all starts. That's a huge responsibility. Kindergarten is where the kids learn to play School. We're all trusting them to do their job well, because if they don't it makes ours harder. I don't want to teach pencil holding and line standing and hand raising.

I am very upfront with my students about my expectations of them and how I feel they reflect on me. I tell them that when they get in trouble in the lunchroom, that makes me look like a bad teacher. If they act up in the library other adults ask why Mr. Robertson's class can't control themselves. Everything falls to me. It means I haven't taught them correctly. I don't tell them to tell their parents to help them behave better. "Go home and tell your mom to teach you how to sit in an assembly!" I don't tell them I have different expectations because this and that is happening at home. I tell them I take their choices personally. When they do well I'm proud of them. When they do poorly I'm disappointed. Either way, I feel it in myself. I tell them this because I want them to see I believe in taking personal responsibility too.

I will defend every idea I have about teaching and every choice I make in my classroom. What happens in my classroom happens because I want it to. That's an important thing to remember. At the end of the day I'm the one making the lesson plans. The grade level has things we need to cover. The principal has goals for the school. The state has tests and trainings and benchmarks. The nation has rankings and policies that come and go. As a teacher I have to hear all of those things. I have to try and make all of those things work in the reality of my room. It can be overwhelming to think about. Teachers are at the very bottom of a very tall tree, and a lot of things fall on us from different heights. There's not much we can do. Can't fight gravity.

What I can do is choose what's important. That might not be the best attitude about the Powers That Be above me, but it makes my classroom work. No one but me is in my room every day. No one but me knows my students, their idiosyncrasies, quirks, and keys. My job, first and foremost, is to create valuable, free-thinking student citizens with the ability to live their lives to the fullness that they choose. That's my first priority. And, since I am Grand High Emperor of All and Beyond in my classroom, I am able to act on that priority. I only have to find ways to do it.

Sometimes I hear teachers complaining that their class won't learn something. The whole class is struggling with this concept and what's wrong with them and why don't they get it? I feel that this is not a productive way to look at student learning. If my class doesn't get something after I've taught it that doesn't mean they aren't bright enough. It means I did it wrong. I need to go back and try again. If a big chunk of the class fails a math test that means I taught that chapter badly. A few failing is one thing, but a big group? My fault. I should have done better.

Same goes for homework. A bunch of students not turning in their homework? What am I doing wrong? How can I change my homework policy? I will get into this in more detail during the discipline chapter later on.

Teaching happens on an island. Everyone is alone in their classroom doing their thing their way. At the end of the day it is the kids and I on a journey. Good materials or bad materials. Computers or fifteen year old textbooks that still call Pluto a planet. A million assessments a year or one Big Test At The End. Good parents, bad parents, grandparents, foster parents, no parents. Those are outside forces that I can't control. All I can control is what happens in my classroom. So I do. With an iron will I control it. I take teaching personally because I should. I am doing what I can to help these children move forward in their lives. In ten years they probably won't remember the Hot Spot Theory or how to multiply fractions, but they will remember what I taught them about finding those answers. They'll remember that in the end it's up to them. No one else makes their choices for them. I want them to internalize the idea that they can do things, but it is up to them to try.

I take teaching personally. If I don't, who will?

Doug Robertson

Chapter 3: Teaching Is Performance Art

Some of the most valuable Learning To Teach classes I took in college (the University of the Pacific- Go Tigers!) had nothing overtly to do with teaching. They didn't happen in the Benerd School of Education. They happened across campus, in a different building full of different people who were planning on doing something much less square with their lives. A building full of artists right next to the DeMarcus Brown Theater.

Introduction to Acting was the very first class I took in college. It was Day One Class One at the University of the Pacific, and it was amazing. The professor's name was Jeffrey Ingman and he was very much an **Acting Teacher**. I took the class because it was one of the branches on the required courses tree. It was probably that or something that looked incredibly boring, so I ended up in Intro to Acting. I'd always been interested in theater anyway, and I loved going to shows, so I figured it couldn't hurt. I jittered in my seat waiting for College to start.

Then this tall, trim, young-looking man with glasses bursts into the classroom shouting, "What ho, what news?" And my entire idea of what a teacher could be was irreparably shifted.

Every day he greeted us with, "What ho, what news?" Arms cast out, sweeping, charging into the classroom. Mr. Ingman, he told us to call him Jeff, another weird thing about college that I never got used to, was Energy in the classroom. He loved teaching, he loved acting and those two truths oozed from every pore. When he was teaching he was on. In his mind this was not a classroom with desks, this was a raised stage, complete with orchestra pit and proscenium. We were not undergrads taking an acting class to fulfil a credit requirement. We were Actors, and we were treated as such.

I ate it up. Mr. Ingman taught with a verve that reminded me of other teachers that I loved from high school and middle school, but combined it with the stage presence of an experienced thespian. Imagine the stereotypical Actor-guy, give him the confidence to support or even accentuate his small eccentricities, and add the magnetic charisma good actors have either naturally or through thousands of hours of work. He was electric. It was the best class I took that year. I had no urge to leave education and join a theater troupe, but I knew I wanted to watch Jeff Ingman teach as much as possible. I knew that I was learning something I wouldn't get anywhere else. I told him as much during our end of the semester conference.

This actually leads to one of those moments in my life that I wish I had back. It's a small thing, but I'll always remember it. In our conference I told him I really loved watching him teach and I was going to be taking the Intermediate Acting the next semester because I enjoyed his class and felt like I was learning a lot about not only acting but teaching as well. We had a great conversation. It built a good interpersonal connection between us on both a student-actor/teacher level but also on a student-teacher/teacher level.

Then I had to go and ruin it by trying to play down how much his class meant to me the next semester. One of the first days of class Jeff went around the room asking people why they were there and when he got to me I said some stupid thing about enjoying the Intro class and so I decided to take this one. Nothing about learning to teach, nothing from the conversation he and I had had just a few weeks before. I'll always remember the look he gave me. It felt like a, "Oh, I see. You're one of those people in front of a group." Out loud I think he said something like, "Oh, that's interesting." I immediately felt terrible but the moment was gone. I never really apologized to him. So now I want to make it formally known in my very own book that Jeff Ingman was an integral part of my growth as an educator and I followed him from class to class whenever I had a hole in my schedule because he inspired me to try new things and to treat my classroom like a stage. He left the University of the Pacific before I graduated to go back to acting for a while, and I'm sure he did great, but I honestly hope he's teaching again.

Thank you, Mr. Ingman.

It was teachers like Jeffrey Ingman that taught me teaching is a performance art. We are actors. If I designed a teaching program for a university I would make a beginning acting class a requisite. What are we doing if not acting? The skill sets are very similar. We have to memorize dialogue. We have an audience, possibly with us, possibly hostile, possibly only there to get out of the rain for a while. We have to keep the audience interested in what we have to say. We have to make complicated things comprehensible for the people in the way back of the room. And we have to do the same show over and over without getting bored. Good actors connect with the material. Good teachers might not connect with multiplying fractions, but they know how to make it look like multiplying fractions is an interesting, amazing, important thing.

Discipline is acting. Teachers are always covering emotions, masking emotions, or lowering an emotional intensity as the scene, excuse me, situation demands. I try very hard to never show my students that I am angry with them. Anger is not an emotion I use in my classroom if I can help it. The only thing they learn from anger is fear. Am I perfect? No, of course not. And, to be honest, there are times, rare times, when I want the child to know I'm angry. Not frustrated, not disappointed, not irritated, but outright and full-on angry with them. Takes a lot. Takes a level of disrespect and bullying towards another student that hurts to see. And even then I'm acting because if I show a student I'm that angry on the outside then on the inside I'm erupting. There are words bouncing around my brain they've never heard before in hyphenated combinations that would set hair on fire. Most of the time, though, when I'm angry with a child I show them disappointment or frustration. These are emotions a child can learn real lessons from. Especially if I've built the proper relationship within my class.

It is not all negative emotions. As I've stated and stated and will continue to state, I'm all about positive emotions in my room. I want the kids to be happy. I want my room to be a place of safety and light in their lives. Sometimes I'm not feeling that, but it should be true anyway. My bad day should not equal their bad day. So I act happy. I pretend to be interested in the story about their cat. I do care. I care very much what happens in my students' lives, but sometimes I have so many other things going on that I really don't want to hear about it right at that minute. But I'll stop and listen. Actually, I'll tell them to hold the story until recess or the bell, then I'll stop and listen. Sometimes, yes, I fake interest. It happens. You can't be 100% present all the time, but you can make the students feel like they are important even when they might not be at that moment.

I act in class when the kids are funny. You cannot laugh at your students. You can't. Students do things all the time that in the back of your mind you want to bend over, point, and howl. Kids are funny. Kids are awkward. Kids are strange. Ask a group of nine year olds to do 25 jumping jacks. I guarantee you will hurt yourself not laughing. Their arms and legs aren't fully connected to their brains yet. It is hilarious.

Thou Shalt Not Laugh At Thy Students. Destroys trust, destroys confidence. Sometimes a student is legitimately funny in class. Sometimes I laugh with that, sometimes I don't. Depends on how the day is going. If the day is going badly they won't get a smile out of me. They need to know Serious

Time is Serious. But if we're having a relaxed educational day and someone cracks a joke, I'll chuckle. Sometimes I laugh outright. Sometimes I can't help it, things come out of nowhere and strike me as hilarious.

Be warned, Reader, that most Funny Classroom Stories fall under the heading of You Had To Be There. This is one of those stories.

I had given the students an assignment about the planets. They had to choose a planet and write a tourism brochure for it with the goal of convincing aliens to come visit, using the information they had learned from their research. Of course one of my sillier kids ended up with Earth. She was doing fine, going along in her presentation, hitting all the good facts, making bad jokes that only landed with the class because third graders will laugh at just about anything. Then, out of nowhere, in a very matter-of-fact voice, she says, "And aliens, please remember, the best parking is in the forest. Lots of space."

It slayed me. It was one of those things that you hear it and it nails you right in the funny bone. The mix of how she said it, where it came in her presentation and the idea of giving parking advice to aliens gelled perfectly for me and I laughed out loud. There may have been desk pounding. I don't know why. I can't explain it. I know it really isn't that funny. I know you aren't laughing right now. You might have smiled. I cracked up. Making the teacher laugh, by the way, is the goal of all class clowns. Making your classmates laugh is easy. Getting to the grown-up is winning a special prize. She practically did a victory dance with her eyes. I was not a good actor then.

Teachers have to make math interesting. I am not a math guy. When I was in school I hated math. No, I haaaaaaaated math. I was not good at it until I had to start teaching it, and then I was a day or two ahead of the class sometimes. I subbed in a middle school once and had to teach two weeks of higher level algebra. A math class I had once upon a time passed, but forgot most of right after the last test. Not in their minds. I am the teacher, I know all this. The students know I must know all this because I am the teacher.

All praise be to the teachers edition.

I would look at the problem, if I couldn't figure it out I'd look at the answer and work backwards. "Ok, so the answer is 72. How could 72 be...hmmm, so if I do this and then this...hey look 72! Awesome." Sometimes I would have no idea where the answer came from. That's what the smart kid sitting front and center is for. "Angela, why don't you explain to the class how you got 72. Very good job, thank you." Meanwhile, I'm frantically taking notes, making her go back just in case someone in the class didn't understand that last step.

For those of you shocked I couldn't do this math and I was a credentialed teacher I can only say that our profession expects our knowledge to be both wide and deep. As a sub I would be teaching drama in middle school one day, then second grade, then sixth grade, then middle school math, then kindergarten. That's a schizophrenic week. Teachers don't get really good at teaching until we have our own classroom and some stability. Some time to get familiar with the material and dig in deeply. To experiment and refresh memories. Teaching methods classes at university are mostly theory and technique. In school we take a little bit of everything, but you never have operational recall of all of it. You have to act like you do.

When an actor is on stage mid-scene and they blank on a line the play doesn't stop. They fake their way to the next bit of dialogue and they do it in a way that the audience doesn't notice. You can't stop, pull out a script, find your place, then say, "Ok, time-in!" You push through, doing some improv along the way. Teachers are improvisors. Teachers are actors. That doesn't make teaching a performance art, though.

Teaching is art because there are no rules, an idea I will explore in more detail later. Teaching requires us to always be present with our classroom. To engage and respond and be interesting. Acting is listening. So is teaching. So is learning. If a teacher tells you that student should be interested and checked in because that's his job then that teacher has never sat in a presentation in their life. They have never suffered through boring, dry, endless lectures that actually slow time down. My job is to impart information, yes. But it is to impart information in a way that makes it stick. "You can lead a child to knowledge but you cannot make him think." Robert Heinlein, *Starship Troopers*. Teachers have to make a child want to think. We have to engage 25 different people on a personal level. We have to make them want to come with us on the educational journey, that is our responsibility. I do it by acting. I treat my classroom as a stage.

One tool in an actor's bag of tricks is the no-take. In professional wrestling it's called a no-sell, when one guy in tights gets punched in the head but forgets to fall down. It's the Blank Look. I love the Blank Look. I use it all the time. It is so much better than verbally correcting a child. Call out without raising your hand and I might not say anything, but I'll stare blankly at you until you realize what you've done. I insist my students say "please" and "thank you" in class. So when they ask me for something and don't ask politely I become a mime. Hand to the ear. Eh? I thought I heard something but I cannot be sure.

When the students complain I make sure that they act. There is no simple complaint. Everything must be as dramatic as possible. This cuts down on complaints. You cannot simply say, "Mr. Robertson, that's a lot of questions." You have to, and I promise I tell them this, put the back of your hand to your forehead, sigh, and say with proper Dickensian misery, "Mr. Robertson! This is sooo many questions!" To which I'll reply, "Yes it is. Get to work."

Drama doesn't make their complaint more likely to sway my decision, but it does make it much less irritating. Sometimes I'll make a child stamp his or her little foot while they complain. Every complaint carries more weight when accompanied by a foot stomp. You feel better afterward too. Try it later when you notice all the cookies are gone again. Make a little frustrated squeak when you do it too.

When a child says, "Mr. Roberson, how do you spell this word? What does that word mean?" I'll look tortured. "Oh," I'll exclaim, hand to forehead, "If only someone would invent a book of words! A book with all the words. Then I could have a whole bunch of them in the room over by those giant red books. Hey, wait a minute..." It is so much more fun than telling the child to get a dictionary. They remember it better too.

When I teach I explore what performers call levels. Levels are best described as high, middle, and low. Those denote where your body is in space. I am a moving teacher, I don't like to park and bark. I'm constantly walking the room, making student eyes track me. Easier to see who isn't paying attention when you're moving. Whose head isn't moving along? I'll get low, kneel down right by a child. I'll get high, I have been known to stand on desks. Someday my principal will walk in on me standing on a desk, waving a yardstick around like a sword, reading from the book. I hope he doesn't mind.

I also constantly adjust volume. The best advice I ever got, and advice that I'm terrible at remembering, is lowering my volume to keep their attention. Make the students lean in to you. Make them try harder to listen. I'm a loud teacher, so I forget this constantly. Until I remember and suddenly I'm Nic Cage. Nic Cage, for those of you who don't know (and for shame), has two acting gears. Quiet, softly crazy Nic Cage.

And LOUD SCREAMINGLY CRAZY NIC CAGE.

Keeps the kids on their toes.

Reading aloud is one of my most favorite things about teaching. There are so many fantastic books out there. If you view teaching as performance art, and you view reading aloud as part of teaching, then your read alouds become chapter-long daily plays. I do voices, I do expression, I get into it. Sitting and listening to someone read from a book can be torture. Acting when you read brings the book to life. When you bring a book to life the students see that reading is more than words on a page. Reading is an adventure. I expect my students to read with expression and I model that every day. I go for it so that they feel safe about going for it. I act silly and shout and whisper and do awful accents because I want them to take risks in class.

We have a monster puppet in my class. His name is Toof. I have a monster puppet in my class because I found him at Target and needed to justify his purchase because he somehow found his way into the cart. Toof is one of the best things I've ever bought for my room. He's a little furry green hand puppet. He's named Toof because he's got big plastic teeth and because it allows me to call Toof time Toof Telling and I like plays on words. I introduce Toof after Christmas break. I tell the students that Toof cannot talk because monsters can't speak human. But they can throw their voices telepathically. So when I'm holding Toof I'm talking for him. When they are holding Toof they are talking for him. This is why Toof's voice sounds different with different people. Each student takes Toof home for two days, at the end of which they present one written page about what they did together, and a picture. I encourage stretching of the truth. Toof loves video games, he attacks cats, he can't swim, and he's not scared of small children (because monsters aren't scared of anything, duh) but he doesn't like them. They have to write the page in first person from Toof's perspective. Then they have to stand in front of the class and have Toof tell us about their time together.

You'd be shocked how into it some of my kids get. They love the chance to play. I'm getting them to practice responsibility, first person writing, art, and public speaking all in one assignment. When I use Toof or Courson, who is a fancier, more expensive monster puppet that only I get to touch, I go for it. I get creative with their voices and their opinions. I take risks and get strange so that the students know it's safe. So they know that's what I want. Puppetry is acting. Jim Henson is a hero.

Great actors take risks. The greatest actors get their audience to emotionally take those risks with them.

Great teachers take risks. The greatest teachers get their students to take risks on their own. Even after they have left your class.

curtain

Chapter 4: Polar Express

The last day of school before Christmas break is one of the dumbest, best days of the school year. You are done (hopefully) with report cards. Students bring in more food than you can possibly imagine. You play games, read stories and watch movies. There is very little related to academics that happens on the last day of school before Christmas break. Why? Because why try and teach? Do you know what teachers ask for for Christmas? We ask Santa to help our kids retain some of what we spent the last four to five months teaching them. Just a bit. Enough so that we don't feel like we are starting completely over when school comes back.

Robin Williams once compared being an alcoholic to having an Etch-a-Sketch for a brain. The same things happens to my kids when they go to recess. I spend all morning drawing carefully, getting the lines right, making sure everything connects. Then they go out to the playground, bounce and shake, and my staircase disappears.

Christmas break is like that, but so much more. They are gone for forever, break lasts so long. Children change so very much over the course of the school year. Sometimes a kid will come back from the weekend and I'll think, "Who are you? What happened? Did you get bitten by a radioactive spider? No? Then get off the walls." By the same token, sometimes they come back and their brains have had the time to digest whatever it was I was trying to teach them and suddenly math tests are being passed, multiplication tables are learned, and reading has expression. These are things that happen to a small person's brain all the time. Constantly evolving, growing, learning, finding ways to make me and every other adult obsolete.

Students can smell break coming. The whole week before break is pretty much a mess. You try to teach because that's your job and there is a ton to do that you haven't gotten to yet because you (*read: I*) just looked at the standards again and oh my god I completely forgot about that because I was teaching this and oh no read this chapter NOW! Even in a well behaved class you can sense their noses twitching. Time off, it is coming, it is almost here, smell that? Like sharks with a drop of blood in the water. Like raccoons and half a pizza in the garbage. Like teachers with free coffee and donuts in the break room. They know. By the day before the last day even the best behaved kids are vibrating in their seats. So we spend the last day gorging and watching movies.

I have a method for approaching Christmas. I have Three Favorite Christmas Books and I read them the three days leading up to break. Three days out from break I read *Olive, the Other Reindeer*. It cracks me up, the word play and onomatopoeia is hilarious. Also, it's a great Intro for teaching onomatopoeia, something kids love to learn because that word is about as much fun to say as any word in the English language. Weeeeeeeeeeee!

The day before break I read my second favorite Christmas book, *Polar Express*. The illustrations are some of the best in children's literature, the story is simple and fun, and the movie associated with it is actually pretty good. Sometimes, if my class has been good, we watch the movie that day. I normally save it for the next day though.

The last day of school before break is, as I've said, a bacchanalia (shout-out to <u>A Christmas Story</u>!) of snacks, reading, and movies. We've pushed the desks out of the way because over break they will be cleaning my room, so everyone is on the floor. There is something about gathering a class together on the carpet that just feels right. It feels like Christmas trees smell. I tell students that they can bring in food as long as it is enough for everyone. Mom can't homemake things because we don't trust people so it has to be store bought. And whatever kind of healthy eating I'm trying to do goes out the window. I don't know how children do it, but they will continue to eat as long as you continue to put food in front of them. They bring in so much food that sometimes I don't know how to spread it out during the day. There's no way we are going to get to all of it. We snack before recess. We snack between recess and lunch. They eat lunch. Then they come back and want more food! It is gastrointestinally amazing. I'm normally pretty good until recess, then my willpower breaks like a cheap pencil sharpener and I can't walk by the end of the day.

On this, the last day, I read my most favorite Christmas book. There can be only one. You must know what it is. It is The Christmas Book. *How the Grinch Stole Christmas*. Dr. Seuss is, in my opinion, the greatest American writer of all time, and the Grinch is one of his most wonderful creations. It also comes with a fantastic movie. Not the Jim Carrey mess, you shall not mention that in my presence. No, the cartoon from 1966, with Chuck Jones' whimsical animations and the best Christmas songs of all time. Right now, as you read this you are going to begin humming "You're a mean one, Mr. Grinch..." It's going to be in your head all day now. You're welcome. As a bonus, the cartoon is only about 25 minutes long, which means if I time it right I have time to read the book, show the cartoon, then show The Polar Express afterwards. All this video time gives me the breathing room to maybe finish stuffing report cards or inputting them maybe if I'm not on top of it, not that I'm not. Maybe.

Each year, after The Polar Express ends I feel bad. I haven't done anything truly educational all day. I should. My kids can learn something today. I have the time for a short lesson. So I do the easy go-to for teachers who just read a book and then showed the movie. Time to Compare and Contrast! There was a year this lead to one of my favorite classroom stories of all time.

The Polar Express had finished and I decided to be educational. I took the book, it's a big hardcover, and the DVD case and I put them side-by-side on the whiteboard. I looked over my class, full to the brim with cookies and brownies and chips and whatnot, and I said, "Ok, let's compare and contrast these two! We will start with differences. What is different about them?" I gesture broadly to the book and DVD behind me.

Hands shoot into the air. My class likes to participate. I spend a lot of energy making everyone comfortable and safe, encouraging them to speak up. The enthusiasm is heart-warming. Down in front is one of my special education kids, waving his hand around with as much verve as anyone else. This is the child that convinced me the Bon Jovi song, "Livin' on a Prayer" is actually called, "Livin' on a Player."

"No, Mr. Robertson, listen closer. 'Woah ohhh, we're halfway there. Woah ohhh, livin' on a player!' See? 'Livin' on a player!' That's the words." I lost that argument and now that's all I can hear when the song comes on the radio.

He doesn't get to participate as much because he's normally pulled out. I like having him answer questions when he's in the room, especially questions he can be successful at. It shows him he can do it, and it shows the rest of the class that he is capable. This is a perfect opportunity to let him answer first, be right, and feel good about himself going into break. So I call on him, "Tell me how these are different."

His chest swells. He answers with confidence, his voice clear and loud. He points to the book and DVD in turn.

"That one's a book. And that one's a movie."

Hmm...

The other hands freeze in the air. I see glances between children as if to silently ask each other, "Wait, is that what he meant?" The boy who answered smiles at me. He knows he's given an excellent response.

So I nod. He is right, after all. It's not his fault I phrased the question unclearly. He gave what is the most obvious answer in the world. He's proud of himself. I'm not going to crush that, what kind of a teacher would do that? I say, "Yes. Yes, you're right. Not what I meant, but you're right. Does anyone else have another answer?"

I let someone else give a more exact answer, more like what I was originally expecting. The train goes over a frozen ocean and almost falls in. The characters talk. There are songs. When they come in the boy realizes what I meant and he dives back in, this time being more right.

He wins again.

Doug Robertson

Chapter 5: Distractions

Teaching is managing distractions. It is rolling with unavoidable distractions and going around avoidable ones. One of the things veteran teachers get better at over time is smelling distractions a long way off. We have a Spidey Sense. A child walks into the classroom and you can tell that today she is going to be a potential distraction. You head that off at the pass (*I hate that cliche*) by going over to her and talking to her before the day begins. I've avoided many class-rocking issues simply by talking to the student who will instigate them, whether that student knows it or not. It's a feeling. Find out how her morning was, see if anything is bothering her. It's a release valve, letting the pressure out when it's low rather than allowing it to build.

Experienced teachers know when regular school goings-on are going to be distractions, and what level distraction they are going to be. An awards assembly is a low-level distraction. It will rile the kids up for a few minutes before and a few minutes after. But if Ronald McDonald is coming to the school to give an anti-bullying talk? Steel yourself and prepare your children. At my school we had a group of strongmen come do a demonstration for the school. The guys who rip phonebooks in half, bend metal rods over their heads, crush an apple in their hands, that kind of thing. At the end they did four and a half minutes about bullying. It was ridiculous. I don't think administration got what was advertised. That's a huge distraction. It also falls into the unexpected distraction range too because I knew there would be an assembly and I prepared my students for that, but I had no idea they would be hooting and hollering and winding the group up like they did.

The key to dealing with expected distractions is to talk to your class. Get them ready for the distraction so it isn't as novel as it might be. Whenever we have an assembly I always say the same thing to my kids.

"What do I expect in the assembly?"

Hands raise. "You expect us to be quiet."

"Yes, what else?"

"Polite." "Well behaved." "Don't play around." "Be respectful." "Don't touch other people."

It should be obvious we have had this conversation before. We have. A lot. I believe that you cannot be mad at your class for doing something if you didn't tell them not to do it first. There is a difference between telling nine year-olds to "be good" and telling them specifically what you expect. I make my expectations very clear. Clear as the water off Hawaii's shoreline. So clear that if a child does misbehave they know exactly why they are getting in trouble, without a doubt, without question. Keeping a class in line can be broken down as simply as-

- Tell them what you're going to do.
- Tell them what you're doing.
- Tell them what you did.

I'll repeat, that's a very simple break down. But it's a good set of guidelines. Some adults shy away from it because it seems like you're treating students like they are stupid. I don't see it that way. I think it means you're being explicit, which is what small humans need to fully understand something. Big humans too on occasion. I would feel terrible if, correction- I have felt terrible when I've jumped on a child for doing something I didn't tell them not to do. Some teachers will say, "Yes, but the child should have known not to." How? How can you be sure? Maybe they didn't know. Maybe that's not in their brains yet. Maybe it doesn't happen that way at home. Maybe this is a completely new and novel situation. It is not hard to spend a few minutes and remove all doubt in your Teacher Brain that the child doesn't know what your expectations are.

Tell them what you're going to do so they can prepare themselves. Go over what you expect to be happening while you're doing it. Be clear. Let them ask questions.

During the course of whatever you're doing check in with them. This is easy during a lesson, hard during an assembly. During an assembly checking in can be something as subtle as eye contact or as blunt as wading through the mass of seated children for a shoulder tap. Eye contact is what I prefer, and it isn't as difficult as all that. Children will look at you before they misbehave. They will check in to be sure you aren't watching. If you can catch that eye you can prevent the behavior. New teachers don't have the skill, but anyone who has been teaching for a few years has the Teacher Eye and the Teacher Look. So much can be communicated with The Look. I've stopped children running across the playground with a Look.

I learned to look for child eyes lifeguarding. Before a child starts to drown they will look directly at the lifeguard. I've seen it dozens of times. Kid floats a little too far past the rope and is suddenly out of their depth. They will lock eyes with the person sitting in that tower. You've never seen eyes like that, wide like saucers, communicating so much. Just eyes above the surface. Just for a moment before the struggle starts. Misbehaving children do the same thing, and like the drowning child they are still checking to see if they are being noticed, just in the other direction.

What I like to do when they don't notice the Look is stare at the offending child. Children can hear a stare. Think of it as The Look Level 2. The misbehaving child might be too absorbed in his pencil drums to notice, but the kid next to him sure does. She looks at me to make she she's not the target, tracks my eyes back to the boy next to her, and it's elbow to the ribs time. A hushed, "Mr. Robertson!" in his direction is all it takes to wake him up. Big eyes in my direction. If I'm lucky I'll even get the Big Gulp of Fear. Behavior corrected. I'll talk to him about it later.

After the assembly I talk to my class again. We debrief. Normally I tell them how wonderful they were. My expectations are very high, and I've told them that. I've told them that I don't expect them to be a good class. I expect them to be The Best Class. I want, what my dream is, is for the presenter to find me after the assembly and tell me that my class was the most wonderful audience they've ever had. Set the bar high. Why not? What's the worst that can happen? They strive to meet my expectation and fall short. But short of The Best Class Ever is still an extremely well-behaved class.

I begin setting up these expectations for dealing with distractions immediately. I train my students to sit in their chairs, to roll with changes, to be flexible and understanding. It helps that I am not the most organized teacher in the world. I'm not the most organized teacher in my school. Often, I'm not the most organized person in my classroom. That means things change all the time. Weird Happens. It doesn't take long for my class to learn that and to bend with the wind. Why? Because I've made it clear from the beginning that I am that kind of teacher. That sometimes things might get a little strange. I like it that way, and I will teach that way for as long as they let me.

But as soon as they demonstrate they can't handle it the strange stops. If they can't go from silly to straight up in five seconds then silly goes away. Plenty of warning, I tell them what I'm going to do, and I'm willing to follow through. Children don't want a Super Serious Classroom. They want flexibility. They want learning to be fun. And they will do whatever they can to hold on to that, especially if they have been explicitly told what it is they need to do. Make it easy for them.

When those parameters are set up and in place strange distractions aren't so bad. They will still ruin the flow of your teaching, but they won't ruin the whole day. Schools are places where the unpredictable happens all the time. That is the result of having a large number of children of various levels and backgrounds collected in one place. A place where nature also exists. Nothing ruins a lesson like nature.

I have had birds fly through my classroom and perch on a stack of books. You could be Jaime Escalante, you are not getting anyone to focus on fractions with a bird in the room. That bird will be the center of attention until you can get it to fly away. How does one get a bird to fly out of a room? This wasn't a class in college. It wasn't a lesson. I took no Avian Distractions 101. I don't want to chase it around the room with a yardstick. What if I hit it on accident? Do you want to murder or cripple a bird in front of your class? I don't want to run at it wildly waving my arms and making hooting noises. What do birds, and most other animals, do when they are startled? Yeah, I don't need to be cleaning that up, adding to the already ruined lesson. The best thing to do, it turns out, it to shut all the windows, turn off the lights, and open one door. The bird should fly to the light. Should. Otherwise I'm taking my class outside. I'm giving up the room to the bird. He wins. We yield.

I hate flying bugs. They are unpredictable. Moths, butterflies, grasshoppers, giant freaking cockroaches, ick ick ick. Hate them. They make me want do a little hand-waving high knees dance and run out of the room. But I'm the teacher. I'm the guy who is supposed to be Totally Cool in this situation. Not only that, but I'm a Man Teacher. Gender norms still exist and as a Man I'm not supposed to freak out at a butterfly flapping around my head. I swallow that down. I stay cool. I chase the offending bug out of the room. The children will either freak and stand on their chairs or gather near the bug to see it up close. No one sits and waits patiently until their Totally Calm And Cool And Not Freaking Out teacher tells them to. Repeatedly. Cockroaches are the worst. In Hawaii those things are huge. They have names and jobs that pay better than mine. They remember you. I vacuumed one up once and I swear I heard it banging on the inside of the vacuum, cursing my mother and threatening my family.

And then there are the children themselves. Children are a huge distraction. Those inside your classroom and out. I tease kindergarteners all the time. I mess up their lines with high fives and faces. They get me back. They troop by my room and laugh through my door. "Mr. Robertson! You're funny! You're weird! Mr. Robertson!" Their teacher lets them. I deserve it. My class of fourth graders snigger. It's funny when kindergarteners are making fun of your teacher. I have to keep them focused and on task. Which is hard when ten tiny faces screwed up with crossed eyes and tongues protruding dance by the door. Of course, kindergarteners aren't the only ones. There are always students walking to the office, or back from the office, or to a pull out class, or back from a pull out class, or to the bathroom (often more of a run, that), or back from the bathroom. They might be running or skipping or talking. Few things are more gratifying than catching a kid running by one door, shouting, "Walk!" out the window, and seeing that same child walking by the time they pass the second door. Gotcha. Smell the brake rubber smoking.

I try to keep in-class distractions to a minimum. My class is trained in behaviors I expect, we work very hard on that through the beginning of the year, and I'm pretty loose about most things. My class is not a quiet one. As long as they are at their desks I'm normally ok. The class knows that. Every lesson I've told them what we were going to do, I told them what we were doing, and we talked about what we did.

Sometimes, though, I've gotten students whose behavior is not always fully under their control. Some students have behavioral problems. That's a thing teachers have to deal with. It's not a judgement or a complaint, it is part of the job. Part of my job is learning to work with those kids and their sometimes random and unpredictable needs. Part of my class's job is learning to deal with and work with other people who might be different from them in interesting ways. These are the times I am most proud of my class.

I had a student in fourth grade who was special needs in a lot of ways. He wasn't in my class for long every day, he spent most of his time in a pull out class. But when he was in class he often made noises. Hooting, repeating, shouting. If disgruntled he'd throw things or be loudly grumpy. I put him in a group by the back door. I talked to the whole class about his needs and what we need to be aware of. I made sure they knew if there was any disrespect shown his way there would be giant problems. They were great with him. They rolled with him. There were days when he was so disruptive he was taken from my room for the day by his aide before it was time, but my class was so calm and good at working around him that I was sure they wouldn't react if a hurricane hit the building.

I've had a student who was overwhelmed by noise and would often end up under his desk. I'd have to coax him out. Or let him work down there. Or let him go outside for a few minutes to calm down. No one complained, "That's not fair! How come he gets to work under his desk? Why does he get to go outside?" They understood. Children care about other children. Children have empathy. Don't let anyone tell you different.

In California I had two boys who were a constant distraction, but for completely different reasons. One was the worst behavior problem I've ever had. No hyperbole. Kicked me, my principal, the special education teacher. He loudly accused me of fornicating with my mother on many occasions. He was a Distraction. There was no getting around him, and rarely could we get through to him. He and I would talk, he and I and the counselor would talk, we would all meet with dad. There would be days where I thought we were getting through to him. He was a smart kid and when he wasn't blindingly angry he did great work. Too often though his past overwhelmed him and there was little we could do. I was reduced to keeping the other students safe and reminding them that when he spun out they needed to do their best to ignore and adapt. He was eventually suspended after I found a homemade double-edged knife in his desk. He'd opened a pair of scissors and wrapped tape around the center as a grip.

The other distracting student was just about as unfocused as I've ever seen. This poor kid would constantly space on what he was doing. This meant that he wasn't a distraction to the whole class, but to the kids around him and to me. I'd constantly be checking in on him, seeing what he was doing and if he was progressing. One story stands out best as a way to illustrate this student's level of distractibility.

We were doing quiet desk work. Everyone's heads are bent over their papers, pencils scratching away. I'm working at my desk. I look up. This boy is standing by the class library. The class library is nowhere near his desk. It is on the opposite side of the room from his desk. There is no path he might have been taking, to the pencil sharpener, to the trash can, to the door, which would have taken him past the class library. I called his name to get his attention. He started, blinked, and looked back at me. "What are you doing by the library?" I asked. He gave me the strangest look. It said, "What are you talking about?" Then he looked back at the class library. I swear the face he made next screamed, "Wait a minute, I am by the class library. How *did* I get over here?" He shrugged and tottered back to his desk. I couldn't even scold him. I'm not sure it was his fault. To their credit, no one in my class laughed.

Tell them what you're going to do.

Tell them what you're doing.

Tell them what you did.

Tell them explicitly at every step what you expect out of them. Do those things and your class will be able to cope properly with any distraction, from a bird flying through the door to a bird flying off a child's finger.

Doug Robertson

Chapter 6: Student Teachers

I've often said that I would be everyone's least favorite administrator. I am positive there would be teachers on my staff that wouldn't like me, and for a year my transfer request inbox would be high and leaning.

One of the reasons would be my feelings on student teachers. I would strongly suggest to my staff that once every three or four years everyone who has the experience should have a student teacher in their class. I wouldn't make it a requirement. I also wouldn't be a passive aggressive Chotchkie's manager asking about flair levels. I would tell my teachers I think that having a student teacher in your classroom, even for one semester and only twice a week, is one of the most valuable experiences a teacher can have. It does two very important things. First, it forces the teacher to reflect and justify everything he does in his classroom, because he has to explain it to the student teacher. Second, it moves the profession forward. Everyone is a student teacher before they are a teacher. A good experience is invaluable to a young teacher's development. Their first year alone in the classroom is going to be hard, but having strong experiences student teaching will go miles towards easing that pain. I had a Mentor Teacher named Jen Thomas who taught me a lot. So much so that when I was having trouble once I started subbing we would go to dinner so I could pick her brain.

I was exposed to a whole new viewpoint when I started student teaching. Suddenly I went from being treated like a student (read: adolescent) to being treated like a peer (read: adult). I got to go into the teacher's lunch room! I could see behind the curtain. I walked through the office, right in like I owned the place, and no one stopped me! These are big things.

As a male in an elementary school there is another thing I quickly had to get used to- teaching, at least in the lower grades, is primarily a female profession. I knew that from my education classes, but sitting in college classes filled with girls and walking into the teacher's lunch room and being fixed by fifteen pairs of laughing female eyes of all ages is completely different. I'm not at all saying I was made to feel uncomfortable because my gender, there is no sexual politics happening here. Though on my first day in the teacher's lounge, I'm the only man present remember, one of the older women looked at me and laughed, "Get ready for a massive dose of estrogen." That's a unique and instructive introduction to a new job.

I took on a student teacher in my sixth year of contracted teaching, my fifth year in Hawaii. I was in my second year teaching fourth grade, and by that point I was feeling pretty confident in my skills. I could run my room on automatic and felt like I had my teaching philosophy and style pretty well nailed down. I actually had been dying to have a student teacher for a while for a very simple reason. I want to help. I love helping. Part of my long long term plan when it comes to teaching is to someday get my Masters then, after I've been in the classroom for twenty years, become a college professor and teach teachers. I like the idea of shaping students for a while, then shaping the people who shape students. I feel like I have an unique and interesting outlook on the entire profession. Heck, I'm writing a book about it aren't it?

This idea of taking the future into my own hands stems from my history as a lifeguard for the City of Palmdale. We had a very low turnover rate from summer to summer as many guards would come back from wherever they were during the year to work at the pools. From that was grew a Veteran/Rookie system. I take no credit for this, guards like Brian Yepp and Mark Thibault created and perfected the system. When you began you were, obviously, a rookie. After your second year guarding you became a vet, an experienced member of the guarding caste system. It was expected that you knew the philosophy of the pools and the way things worked. We had specific ways of doing things and specific ways of thinking about the job of lifeguarding.

As a vet you were given a rookie, a new lifeguard or pool aid, and your job would be to help them become the kind of person we wanted at the pool. You were to do this without them knowing that you were their vet. Rookies were not told this vet/rookie system existed. Everyone helped everyone else, but you helped your rook a little more. You spent a little more time with your rook. You were expected to be sure they were on with their skills. I had a rookie one year that was a weak swimmer. Great guy, strong on the skills and classroom stuff, excellent attitude, not a good swimmer. He and I would work in the morning, after training, between swim lesson sessions, at the end of the day, every opportunity we had at making him a better swimmer and by the end of the year he was hanging tough. He later became the manager of one of the pools. I do not take full credit for this by any means, but I like to think I had a part. The vet responsibilities extended beyond the pool as well. Was your rookie partying a little too hard? Talk to him, get him straightened out. Even after the summer was over everyone was supposed to stay tight. Have you burned your rookie this month?

I took many things from my summers at the pool and feeling responsibility for the future was one of those. If you want something done right, do it yourself, then train other people to do it that way too. Naturally, I was thrilled when a professor from the University of Hawaii came to our school asking after mentor teachers. I put my hand up right away. I had my hand up before she finished asking the question. Oh, oh, Mr. Kotter. A chance to mentor a young teacher, to train them in the ways of the Force through my eyes? Yes, please!

Not many other teachers had my zeal. I'm not

condemning them, we are a busy bunch and for many having one more thing on their plate is too much. I personally don't think that's a good excuse. I think it is our responsibility as veterans to jump at the chance to help new teachers. Plus, you could see how much the UH lady needed people. She had the look of someone who gets told no a lot. That's too bad.

Hence, were I a principal, why I would direct my staff to take on student teachers. You're helping yourself, the future, and our colleagues in the college ranks. Teaching is not insular. A big buzzword right now is staircased curriculum. Looking at how each grade connect to the previous and next. Taking on a student teacher is seeing that staircase all the way through to its logical end.

I have, if you can't tell yet, very strong opinions on how teaching should be done. I recognize that my ways are not the best ways nor are they the only ways. I think they are damn good ways though. Taking on a student teacher would be my chance to put those ideas to the test. Does this translate to another person? Am I a crazy man alone in my room, or will a fresh pair of eyes see what I see? I knew I would have to get lucky with my assigned student, but I welcomed the challenge. I like saying yes to things and then figuring out how to make that yes work. Run the committee? Sure! What does PBS mean? Organize a Christmas pageant? Ok! The first thing I needed to do was crystalize for myself and for my student teacher exactly how I thought about teaching. I needed a list.

I present now the list I wrote for my student teacher. I bought her a journal to use in the classroom, because presents make people feel welcome, and this is what I wrote on the first page of that journal.

1. DON'T PANIC!
2. Remember: They are children.

3. Discipline the behavior, not the child.

4. Your classroom will reflect you, for good or bad.

5. When in doubt- The Beatles.

6. Steal- Others have already taught this.

7. Learn from them, laugh with them.

8. Fear may motivate, but love inspires.

9. They will rise to your expectations, but they may also need a boost.

10. Why blame the parent? You aren't teaching the parent.

11. Say please and thank you. You are the example now.

12. Sometimes allow yourself to be amazed someone trusts you with all these tiny people.

13. Volunteer to coach, help, and lead.

14. Speak up in meetings, and have faith in your own opinions. Rock the boat. Promote change.

15. Try not to complain about your kids too much. Negativity is sneaky and contagious.

16. Ok, sometimes you can blame the parents.

17. Be prepared and be comfortable.

18. Be able to justify everything you do.

19. Don't worry, the teacher next door is faking it too.

I will readily admit that some of those are very warm and fuzzy, some are very general, and some run contrary to many teachers' beliefs. That's fine. I think these 19 things can guide a teacher through whatever kind of day they are having. I stand by every single one of those notes. I gave the journal to Bethany, my student teacher, and over the next few days when we would talk about teaching I would also talk about the list. I went through it one by one with her, she asked questions and I explained why each belonged on the list, gave examples, and justified each note's existence. I told her that if she followed these things she and I would have a great semester together.

Bethany and I got on like gangbusters. I could not have

been more lucky. She worked hard, she was smart, she listened to me go on and on, and she came prepared to work. The first semester of her student teaching was set up so that she would come in two days a week to observe, help, and eventually teach her own lessons. I know some teachers pushed their student teachers to the side. They would have their poor guest sit in the back of the room and watch them teach. Frankly, nothing sounds more boring. I vividly remember my student teaching experiences and while I had an excellent mentor teacher in my second grade placement, Mrs. Jen Thomas, the days where I was to sit and observe were still torture. It's so boring to watch someone else teach. Even when they are good, and even when you are actively trying to learn from them there is only so long a grown body can sit and listen to second grade material, let alone a second grade body.

Keeping that in mind, Bethany and I developed a system. I would have her come in with specific goals, things she wanted to know, things she wanted to watch for, and things she wanted to do in the room. Then together we would aim for those goals. I wanted to move her from purely observing to actually working in front of the class with the students as quickly as possible. You only learn to swim by swimming and you can only learn to teach by teaching. I had to trust her with my class, she had to rise to my expectations. So after a few days observations she started taking over morning work, a short two-sided worksheet I give to my class to start each day. It's easy, and if she messed up something it wasn't a tragedy. Morning work was training wheels. She and I would talk about each question, there are five on each side, one math side and one reading side, going over the answers and how I expected her to talk about them. Then I'd let her teach it. Honestly, correcting morning work isn't intense teaching. But it is speaking in front of a class. It is getting up there, and getting your toes wet. It is terrifying for a person sometimes.

No one wants to make a mistake correcting fourth grade math, you feel like a dope. I make mistakes on math all the time, so don't feel like a dope anymore. Mistakes lead to teachable moments about correcting yourself, another important lesson! But new teachers don't have the confidence yet to make a mistake in front of the class. They already feel like the kids know they don't know what they are doing. Secret- The kids don't know.

Slowly she moved into larger and larger sections of the day, always with my guidance and always talking to me first. My biggest concern was actually about myself, and it was the same concern I had for her when she was observing. How would I keep myself from getting bored? I fully admit to being Shiny Object Distractible. I needed a plan.

So I closed my laptop, grabbed a clipboard and a few pieces of paper, and started taking notes. I created a two-column chart. One column I called Praise and the other I called Corrections. As she taught I would fill the page with observations about what I was seeing. Things I liked, things I wasn't thrilled with, mistakes I saw, ways to improve. At the end of the day we would sit and go point by point over my chart. I'd explain why I liked this but didn't like that, how she did this and how she should do that next time. To her credit she rarely made the same mistake twice. Which was great because it freed her up to make all new mistakes! I love mistakes. I can teach mistakes.

I encouraged her to try new things and indulge her instincts. The only way to build teacher skills is to play with them and see what worked. My only hard and fast rules involved how she treated my students, who I will protect above all else. That was never an issue because she was kind, too kind at the start like all new teachers. The first time you make a child cry you feel awful about it. That goes away quickly. Children cry. That's a thing that happens. They get over it. As long as she wasn't being mean about it, not trying to make them cry, that was fine.

Discipline is what you're learning a lot of the time in the beginning. It's the hardest thing to get right and fine tune, but also one of the most important. I tried to indoctrinate her into my way of thinking about discipline. Thou shalt treat thy children with respect. Thou shalt correct the behavior, not punish thy child.

I gave her the standing assignment of coming in with specific goals I should look for every day to better aim our time together. With this focused approach Bethany and I were able to make great strides quickly and I couldn't have been more pleased with her progress. I feel it allowed her to feel safe with me. We trusted each other enough to know criticism comes from a place of respect and a need to make each other better.

By the end of the semester my whole class was smitten with Ms. Awana and we were all very sad to see her go. I may have given them the goal of making her cry on her last day. It may have worked.

She and I went out to lunch afterwards. Over the course of the semester we had become friends, and I gave her a copy of *Charlie and the Chocolate Factory*. I'm not going to tell you why. That's between the two of us.

The experience had solidified in my mind that I was doing something right in the classroom and I approached the second semester with a new student teacher with vigor. When signing up for a student teacher I had signed up for a two year term, so I was getting someone new after Christmas break. This was even more nerve-wracking than first semester because Bethany had set the bar so high. Added on to that the woman who runs the student teacher program came to me and asked me to take this new guy because he was struggling during his first placement. She thought a male influence would straighten him out and get him back on track.

So when Matt came to me he and I had a very honest talk about expectations. I told him what I wanted, he told me he understood, and that was that. He was late maybe twice, something I sympathized with having had trouble getting up on time as a student teacher myself. But it wouldn't fly in my room. After the second time I told him, "Listen, please don't make me be a jerk about this. Just be on time, and we'll be fine." He was never late again. Honest, open feedback is the best way to teach.

The hardest part of working with Matt was not comparing him to Bethany. I went out of my way not to mention her to him. We did the same thing I did first semester, easing him in and working the two column Praise/Correction chart with him. I'm pleased and proud to say that by the end of the semester Matt was becoming a fantastic young teacher. He was overcoming the struggles of the early semester, I was getting very positive feedback from his UH teacher, and my students were learning.

The second year I begged for and got Bethany back. She would be in the room for the entire year this time and involved in every facet of the classroom. Second semester she would be there every day, and she would solo for three weeks near the end. I would not be allowed in my classroom. That's hard.

Having student teachers is one of the most rewarding things I've ever done in teaching. I love feeling like I'm impacting the future of the profession. I take my job very personally. One of the things I told both Bethany and Matt numerous times is in their classroom they are the bottom line. Everything starts and stops with them. If the whole class is misbehaving then you need to look at yourself. You will never get 25 bad kids. So if it feels like it, what are you doing wrong? You will never get 25 low kids. So if it feels like it, what are you doing wrong? By the same token, I got two excellent student teachers. I must be doing something right.

As a parent I would not hesitate to put my child into Mrs. Edwards's (she got married over the summer) or Mr. Oshiro's classes. They impressed my principal so much that he hired both of them at the end of the year. They are smart, hardworking, and they have a love for the job and for the children that will serve them in good stead. I couldn't be more proud.

Every teacher should have the chance to feel like this. When the professor from UH asked for volunteers for mentor teachers one of my colleagues laughed and said she didn't have anything to teach a student teacher. That nothing about her room was special. I'm about to sound *very* judgemental, but if you feel that way about your job then you are in the wrong job. Everyone does something special, everyone has something to offer the future of their profession.

As an administrator, I would want my teachers to take student teachers. How they reacted to that request would tell me, I think, a lot about them as a teacher. You have the time to strengthen the field. You're a teacher all the time. Spread the word.

Everything that happens in my classroom reflects on me. I tell my students that. I told Matt and Bethany that. If they are bad teachers, I was bad at teaching them. I truly believe they are both going to be fantastic teachers. That does not mean I am a fantastic teacher, but I'd like to think I helped.

Be a part of the solution. Affect change deeply on as many levels as you can.

Chapter 7: Philosophy on Discipline

In my world the purpose of classroom discipline is simple, straightforward, and explicit. All disciplinary actions I take in my classroom are guided by one idea-

The purpose of classroom discipline is to change behavior.

That is it.
That is all.
That seems simple.
But it's not.
You see, that's not what classroom discipline *feels* like it should be about. Changing behavior is too simplistic. That isn't what comes to mind when a person, a normal person, thinks about discipline.

What do you think about when you hear the word discipline? Dictionary.com has definitions like "to penalize in order to train and control; chastise; correct." One of the first synonyms that pops up is punish.

That's wrong.

The purpose of classroom discipline is not to punish. It is to teach, same as the purpose of everything else that happens in the classroom. The student might be punished through the correcting of behavior, but punishment itself is not the goal.

In my class I have an overt discipline plan and a secret discipline plan. The overt discipline plan is simple. It is simple for two reasons. The first is that a simple plan is easy for me to remember and therefore enforce fairly. The second is that a simple plan is easy for my students to understand and remember and therefore follow without problem.

I build the classroom rules with my students on the first day of school. I give them a broad task. I say, "Tell me what rules are important for a classroom." Students immediately

Doug Robertson

begin to call out rules and I write each one on the board.

Raise your hand to speak. Don't run in class. Don't talk while the teacher is talking. Don't play with scissors. Don't fight. Be nice. Share. Don't make fun of people. Don't draw on your desk. Be respectful. Don't steal.

When the tide starts to ebb I ask for more. Surely there are more rules we need to run a good classroom. You can do better! You've been in school for five years.

Listen to the principal. Walk in the halls. Don't throw food in the cafeteria. Turn in your homework on time. Come to school on time. Don't talk back. Don't start rumors. Don't cyberbully (ah, 21st century schools). *Don't eat in class.*

On and on they roll. If you want to be amazed, ask your class to come up with their own rules and punishments. Children know how they are supposed to behave and have way harsher ideas on punishment than I do. I keep them going until I barely have any room left on my board. Then when they have run out of ideas I turn to the class and say, "Ok, here are our class rules for the year. What do you think?"

What do you think they think? They can't believe it. They make the best noises of disbelief; snorts and scoffs and gasps. "What's wrong?" I ask them. "I asked you for rules of a good classroom. I want us to have a good classroom. This is what you said. These are our rules."

"It's so many!" someone will call out without raising his hand (probably the kid who put "raise your hand" on the board).

"Hmm, you know, you're right. That is a whole lot of rules. If I made this our class rules would you be able to remember all of them?" Heads shake in the negative. "But if you can't remember all the rules how will you know if you're breaking one? That's tough. Do we see any rules that say the same thing? Can we cut this list down?"

Together we put the various rules into categories. I know

where all of this is going. I already have my class rules printed, ready to hand out and send home. I don't want to be the one who tells them the rules though. I want them to tell me.

Turn in your work on time folds into Do all your work which gets put under **Be Responsible**. Don't run in the classroom or at school can melt into Don't play with scissors and those end up beneath the **Be Safe**. Don't talk while someone else is talking, Raise your hand, and Be nice become **Be Respectful**. All the other free floating rules magically appear under **Make Good Choices**.

I ask the class if they think Be Respectful, Be Responsible, Be Safe, and Make Good Choices are good classroom rules? Are they easy to understand? Do they cover any behavior issues which might come up? This time the class answers in the affirmative and we spend the next few minutes gaming out different scenarios to see if that's true. I bring up something terrible Stu (who you'll meet in more detail in Chapter 22) might do like pushing a kindergartener down or interrupting me and make a student tell me which of the four rules he's broken. I let them see for themselves that those four guides are all we need in our classroom. "Really," I'll say, "We only need the one. I could leave it at Make Good Choices because that's what all the others are, but I think we need a little more guidance than that, don't you?"

Be Respectful. Be Responsible. Be Safe. Make Good Choices. Four easy to remember rules. Easy for me. Easy for them. Easy rules are important. This way when a child gets in trouble they don't have to look at a list to find out why. There isn't any question. I can explain why they are getting in trouble quickly and simply, in a way that everyone understands.

Another thing I like about the four is that they are positive statements. Ask a child about rules and they will come up with things they shouldn't do. Don't run. Don't talk. Don't spit in your brother's ear. Negative statements. There are ways around negative statements. Well he said I couldn't spit into my brother's ear, but if I lick my finger and stick it in his ear that's different! He didn't say I couldn't do that. Positive statements guide much better than negative. They know what they can do, how they should behave.

Once the rules are in place I tell them what my discipline plan is. We don't build this together. It is set already. Again I use examples of poor behavior. "Let's say Stu talks while I'm talking. See this board in the back of the room? I'm going to tell Stu to write his name down on it." I've got a small white board with How Is My Day written across the top propped up in the back on the room. I write "Stu" on it. I tell the class that Stu is not yet in trouble. A name on the board means he has been warned. I'm big on warnings. Very rarely should harsh discipline fall out of the sky onto a child's head. I believe children should be given every opportunity to correct their own behavior before I have to step in. A name is a warning that tells Stu he's crossed a line. He writes his own name because I want him to be sure he knows. Also, he writes his own name because I'm not interrupting my lesson any more than I have to. I've got too much to teach to be walking to the board every time someone speaks up. He can write his name, let him do it.

At this point I hold up a declaratory finger. "IF! If Stu rolls his eyes at me. If he stomps his little foot. If he grumbles or groans or protests or huffs, he will move straight to the next step. Don't be disrespectful to me. I won't have it. I will not be disrespectful to you, you owe me the same back. Understand?" To make my point I huff and stomp and roll my eyes at the children. I'm being funny, but I'm also showing them exactly what I mean. There will be no question later on. I am being clear.

I go on with the story of Stu's Bad Day and Stu makes another poor choice. Maybe he throws a ball of paper at a classmate or isn't paying attention, things which are disrespectful. I will tell Stu to put a check next to his name. Now Stu is in trouble. But not intense awful terrible trouble. Stu has made poor choices and he owes me sentences.

It is at this point I diverge from many teachers. The expected next step here is to take away recess. I absolutely refuse to take away recess. I won't do it. Losing recess is not an option. It's one of the few places I'm completely inflexible regarding my class. Recess is one of the most important parts of the day for children. Many of our kids are going to go home from school and sit in front of a screen until dinner. They are not going to play like you and I might like. They won't be outside, running around. They need to be. This 20 minute period might be the only running around outside time they get for the whole day.

On top of that, they *need* the break. Sitting in a desk all day is a bummer. Children are full of manic energy. The ones who act up in class the most are the ones who most badly need time to run around the field like a crazy person. I want them to go wear themselves out a little. It makes them easier to deal with when they come back in. On rainy days I can see some kids vibrating from pent up energy.

At the tippy top of all these reasons is one extremely important and selfish one- I want a break. Recess is my break time too. I need to pee. I need to make copies. I need to sit and stare at my computer for 20 minutes and not think about anything at all. I need to put my head on my desk and enjoy the quiet. I need to turn on some music and dance around. Why should I punish myself by keeping a group of children in my room?

Recess might be one of the only things about school those

children enjoy. I want them outside. Sometimes it's one of the only parts of the day I enjoy.

It is at One Check that I explain all that to my class, though not in those terms. I tell them that I don't want to take recess away. I admit, I don't tell them I *won't* mostly because absolutes are dangerous in a classroom. They disallow flexibility. I tell them that at the end of the day, if they remain at one check, they will have extra homework which consists of writing one page of sentences relating to what they did to get the check. It isn't hard. They have to think about the sentence. They have to be responsible. They have to reflect on their behavior. The page is due the next day at the start of the day. If they don't turn it in then they owe me two pages.

This is another place I feel a lot of teachers get it wrong. Look at the last two sentences of that paragraph and extrapolate forward what could happen. Very quickly an irresponsible child could have five pages, ten pages, twenty pages of sentences due to me. What does that solve? Nothing. The child is buried under work so deeply he knows he'll never dig his way out. So why should he try? The child will give up on doing the sentences, and give up on trying not to get into trouble.

More importantly, think about my overriding precept for discipline- Change Behavior. If a child has gotten to twenty pages of sentences, twenty reflections, twenty days of missed recess have they learned anything? Did my discipline work?

No!

If I'm running a plan that allows a child to keep making the exact same mistake which I punish in the exact same way then I'm not really disciplining. I'm only punishing. Nothing is changing. Nothing is getting better. I don't want any of my students to get in trouble. In Fantasy Land I eventually figure out how to keep everyone from needing discipline. It is my responsibility to find ways for them to be successful. If my discipline plan allows a student to get stuck in a negative feedback loop my discipline plan is broken. I tell the class that if they get three sentence pages deep I send a note home and at five we have a meeting with mom and dad and maybe the principal, breaking the cycle of failure.

The plan has one more step.

I continue Stu's story of woe until Stu makes one last mistake. Could be a big one, could be a little one. Doesn't matter. He's getting a second check. As a theater minor I enjoy a little drama in my classroom so I let the second check hang in the air for a few moments while I stare over them. If I could I'd cue an ominous thunder roll. This is the first time they see the Serious Teacher Face. At two checks the student calls home.

"I," I tell them, "am not the one in trouble. I am not calling home. You are. You call your mom or dad at work or at home or on their cell and you explain to them your choices." Depending on the severity of the offenses a trip to the office may also be called for, though I prefer to deal with all problems in-house.

The call home is scary to most children. It works. It's unexpected. Think about yourself as a nine year old, standing by the phone while your teacher has you dial the number. It would be bad enough if the teacher was calling your mom, but you have to do it? Tears, right? Everyone cries.

I don't let children get to two checks very often; I dislike the phone call too, but when I do there are always tears. After the child sobs their explanation into the reciever I take it to further explain if I need to. The student makes the phone call because the student must take personal responsibility for her actions. She tells mom what she did.

After all that I do tell the class that there are ways for them to jump levels. Bullying, fighting, theft: those are serious and will be dealt with quickly and harshly. I will not tolerate my students disrespecting each other. They know there are things that can move them up the chain faster. There are no doubts.

My favorite part comes next. After the revelation of the phone call I let them stew for a minute. I want the thought of calling mom or dad to turn over a few times in their heads. If they think about it now hopefully that will prevent it from actually happening later.

I stand next to the How Was My Day board and ask the class what happens to Stu the next day when he comes into class. They are universally positive he's in for it. I arch an eyebrow and grin. Then I take a paper towel and wipe Stu's name from the board.

"Stu starts over."

The blinks are nearly audible.

Everyone has a bad day. Everyone is allowed a bad day. But the next day is a new day. You start over. Again, I make it clear that there are things which can follow them, bullying chief amongst those. But for the most part, for the issues I expect to deal with over the course of the year, every day is a fresh slate. New chances to make new choices. "Besides," I say, "None of you will get to two checks anyway. Right?" Heads nod. Someone will though. Someone always does. It has to happen so the others can see. But they won't get there today.

Children make mistakes and my discipline philosophy is built on that. I have no problem with children making mistakes. I have problems with repeated mistakes. If my plan doesn't change unwanted behavior then there is something wrong with my plan. It must be flexible. If I need to involve a counselor, if I need to call a parent earlier than planned, if I need to sit and have a real heart-to-heart with the child and ask them to tell me how to help I am free to do it.

I'm very clear about wanting everyone to succeed. I build

relationships in my class which make the students want to succeed for me.

That leads to my secret discipline plan. It's the 5:1 Idea. For every one negative comment I make in my class I need to make five positive ones. Positive reinforcement is a touchstone of everything about my room. My classroom should be a place the students want to be. A place they feel safe. I ignore negative behaviors and praise behaviors I want to see repeated. I try extremely hard to follow my 5:1 ratio. I stole the numbers from the Leeward Positive Behavior Support committee, of which I was a chair at my school for five years. The idea of positive behavior is one I've carried with me since I can remember.

Some teachers seem to love getting on students' cases. It seems like they enjoy tearing students down. The discipline process is fun for them. I worked with a pair of teachers who called themselves Hammer One and Hammer Two. Get in trouble in one room, the other would hammer you too. Back and forth, with pleasure and shouting and ridicule. It made me sick. I spent most of that year eating lunch in my classroom rather than listen to them joyfully complain about children and laugh at how they'd punished them. This is not hyperbole.

When I see something I like I call it out. I dance it. I high five it and do whatever I can to make sure it comes again. Of course I yell at my students, but not very often. Real yelling is like an A-Bomb. You can use it, but you can only use it once or twice. If you're constantly yelling at your class for all manner of problems then they will never be able to tell when you are actually mad and when you're just being your mean self. When I yell my kids know Serious Things Are Happening.

Sometimes I don't yell. Sometimes, when I'm well and truly angry I will stand in front of my class not saying anything. Staring. For a long long time. Uncomfortably long.

Then I'll speak very quietly about why I'm so mad. Quiet is worse than loud. Quiet is scarier. Quiet is unusual. Quiet can convey anger and disappointment and frustration all at once. All in a look. In a breath. I'll give them something to do and tell them they need to be silent until I'm feeling better and I'll sit at my desk to cool off. Can't do that very often either. Don't have to. Quietly mad Mr. Robertson is terrifying. I don't like him either, but he's there.

I know I'm tempting fate by saying this but I've never had a class to complain about. I've had individual students, but never more than two at any one time. I always feel like I've got a good group, a respectful group. We have our little issues, normal things that come up when you put 25 children in a room together, but nothing terrible. I don't complain about my class because I've got a good class. Maybe it's the luck of the draw. Maybe my time is coming.

Maybe, though, when students have a positive classroom environment, when their teacher believes in reinforcing the good and changing the bad, when they hear praise more often than they hear criticism, they become the class you expect them to be.

Your class reflects you, for better or worse.

Chapter 8: When the Students Are Hard You're Doing Your Job

"If it was easy everyone would do it. The hard is what makes it great."
-Jimmy Dugan

Teaching is not an easy job.

No one ever told me it would be an easy job. I don't imagine anyone has ever gone into teaching honestly thinking it would be easy. I don't know how you could. What kind of a person thinks, "25 children in a room with me, and I'm supposed to keep them busy and learning for eight hours every single day for 180 days? No problem." That's before you take into account all the meetings, paperwork, and meetings where you have to do paperwork.

The reality of the classroom is once you hit your groove the act of teaching becomes less challenging. Like anything else, the routine you settle into helps blunt the difficulty level of what you're doing. Add experience to that and soon the actual teaching can become, while not easy, less stressful and overwhelming. Lessons are planned and executed. Grades are taken and recorded. Time flows forward faster than it should.

Teachers think in years. We have to. Next year, assuming you don't change grade levels, you'll be teaching the same thing you taught this year. Maybe you'll change up the How, but the What isn't likely to change all that much. Even with all the changes and modifications to state and federal standards the basic gist of each grade's goals and objectives remains unchanged. A good teacher is a reflective teacher no matter the standards. Reflective teachers look at each lesson as it happens and decide what worked and what didn't work. Then we file those observations away for next year. If the language arts basal doesn't change you can have the stories memorized in a few years. The best part of that is being able to avoid and modify the stories you know are eyelid-droopingly boring. I'm looking at you, non-fiction story about birds.

Schools are constants. The buildings, the books, and often the teachers do not change from year to year.

Students are variables. Every year each classroom gets a fresh influx of pre-adults. New brains, new attitudes, new knowledge, new backgrounds, new chemical mixes. Dealing with that is when teachers shine. Anyone can plan a lesson. Anyone can look at a story in a book and put together some questions. It takes a teacher to look at those lessons and questions and fiddle with them until they match up with the personalities and learning styles that live in his classroom. That is teaching. If you aren't modifying and adapting you aren't teaching. You're standing in front of a group of children talking at them.

Students are the hard part of teaching because students aren't drones or clones or robots. At some point every good teacher realizes that each of the pairs of eyes looking up at her are connected to an individual. Not a number, not a grade, but an actual real live person. It is hard to think of students as individual human people sometimes. Sometimes I just want them to stand in a straight, quiet line and I don't know why they won't. Why won't they just do what I'm asking them to do!? Don't they know I'm the Teacher and they are the Students? I understand how this power dynamic works, why don't they? Why won't they learn these things I'm talking at them about? How do I program this thing? And where is the cursed mute button!?!

Students are frustrating because humans are frustrating. Teachers love to complain about students being frustrating. Complaining is great; it's a pressure release valve and as long as it doesn't become habit that's a fine thing. Too much and it moves from a pressure release to something much more sinister and poisonous.

I think we should welcome the days when the students are hard. We should welcome the lessons that go horribly wrong. I think the days when the students are driving me up the walls, the days where nothing works, are the days when I become a better teacher. I also think I'm a little (read: a lot) masochistic. That's probably important.

I'm a triathlete. That means I enjoy going out for a nice long swim, then getting out of the water, running to my bicycle, and riding for miles and miles. When that is done I change my shoes and run run run. I pay people money to allow me to do this in a group so that I may have a new t-shirt I'm never going to wear from a race I have no hope of winning.

Of course, I don't just show up at the race and expect to be able to compete (or complete it). I spend weeks and weeks training for even the shortest distance triathlon. You can't train for a triathlon inside. (*Full disclosure: You can, but that's not any fun at all and hurts it my metaphor.*) The weather, much like a full classroom (see, this is related), is unpredictable at best and can get ugly at a moment's notice. A training ride that starts with beautiful sunshine might middle with brutal wind and end with a soaking downpour. Wind on a bike is the worst. Cross-winds push me into traffic. Tailwinds are fun, I'm flying down the road. In the back of my head, though, I know that I'm going to have to turn around eventually. Tailwinds are headwinds you aren't cursing at yet. Headwinds make me feel like I'm going exactly 2mph. Headwinds are riding uphill when the road is flat. Don't get me started on climbing. I should hate all these rides. I should only enjoy the clear sky, light cooling breeze rides. Flat, no climbing. With a friend in front of me to draft off of.

But I don't hate the painful rides. Those rides are the best. The rides where I struggle and hurt and have to dig deep are the rides that make the most difference come race day. I seek out steep hills to exhaust my legs on. I enjoy the days on the bike that break me down into little lycra-covered pieces and make me wonder how I'm going to get home. That's when I get mentally tough. That's when I build the suffering reserve that will allow me to push through pain barriers out on the course.

What does that have to do with teaching? Am I really calling my students uphill climbs in a headwind? Sometimes, yeah. Sometimes students are harder than the hardest ride. Sometimes I go to the bathroom just to have a chance to bang my head against the wall for a minute. Those are the days where I become a better teacher.

There are easy days. Easy days come no matter how effective a teacher you are. Times when the whole class is sympatico and the world ticks like a freshly wound watch. I'd argue that more effective teachers have more easy days simply because they are in better control of their class. They're in better shape, to continue the metaphor.

Anyone can teach on an easy day. The class is quiet and no one is playing in their desks. There are no small arguments breaking out over an eraser or who won the basketball game at recess. The whole class looks alert, like they weren't up until all hours playing video games. My coffee tastes like I got the water-to-grounds ratio right for once. Hands are raising with little-to-no calling out and a good answer comes out of the mouth attached to the hand. These are the days I want my principal to come and visit. Those days let me hone the small edges of my craft because I'm not busy putting out fires.

Then there are the hard days. No one, including me, got any sleep last night. No one, including me, ate breakfast. My coffee is either light brown water or tooth-etching sludge. The students are either vibrating out of their seats and hanging from the ceiling fans OR reenacting Romero's classic Night of the Living Dead. No one understood the homework. A gecko, a bird, a bug, and a kindergartener all end up in the room at some point. One of my lights burns out. The projector quits working mid-lesson. A misunderstanding causes me to discipline the wrong kid but he's so upset he doesn't tell me I got it wrong until I catch him silently crying on to his work an hour later. The coffee creates an emergency which has to be taken care of **right now**. And my principal wants to observe without notice.

How well a teacher is able to absorb each of these setbacks tells you a lot about them. Can you roll with broken equipment? Do you have tricks in your bag to wake everyone up or calm them down? Is this the time to drop one of your few A-Bombs? Good teachers have these days and learn from them. I've had days where the bell rings and I banish the students from my class with a, "Go. Go home. I don't want to see any of you until 7:45 tomorrow morning." Then I lie down across a group of desks and watch the ceiling fan until my head stops throbbing. Or I sprint for the parking lot. Most days I'll be at school for at least an hour after the bell. I'm allowed to escape once in awhile.

Once I can think again I assess the day. Maybe it was a full moon. Maybe it was an assembly. Maybe it was just one of those days. I still have to figure out what went so wrong and how I can prevent it. Those are the days when I truly reflect on everything that happened in my classroom. Those are the days when I earn my meager pay. Because my job is to teach students through madness and exhaustion, flickering lights and fire drills, broken computers and lost books. Uphill in the wind is when I learn about myself as a teacher. Hard days are what will make me great.

Doug Robertson

Chapter 9: Dressing Up

I've been a Sneetch at school. I've also been a zombie, a pirate, a biker, a cyclist, a football player, Batman, Professor Snape, and Clifford the Big Red Dog.

Schools are very often serious places with lots of rules and strict dress codes. Depending on the type of school you might be told exactly what you must wear every day or maybe you're just told your skirt is too short and your straps are too skinny. I've never worked at a mandatory uniform school. I don't imagine I would like it, though I've been wrong before. I don't see the need for dictating behavior to that extreme. I feel like it would make the environment more boring. Then again, I know plenty of teachers who don't mind or even enjoy mandatory uniforms. I do think that if you require students to wear a uniform you should provide it. We are not trying to create barriers to entry, and a free education isn't free if a child can't show up without spending money on proper clothes.

I have no problem with the way most students dress. I have a major problem with blaming elementary school students for how they dress. None of my kids work, which means none of them are buying their own clothes. You want to complain about the clothes, complain to the parents. I've seen sixth graders at school with giant pot leaves on their shirts. I've also seen a fourth grader in an "F.B.I.- Female Body Inspector" shirt. They make that in children's sizes? Really? Why? Maybe uniforms aren't so bad. Or maybe these parents should think a little harder when making their couture choices.

Many schools have Spirit Weeks, where their student council comes up with themes for each day and the campus lightens up for the week. Every Spirit Week has stand-bys. Sports Day. Dress Up Day. Pajama Day. I love those days. I don't know if teachers are supposed to dress up. I've never asked permission and I've never been told I couldn't. How could I pass up the chance to dress up for school? That wouldn't be any fun at all.

I've dragged my wife to a dozen stores looking for the perfect hat for Swag Day. First, I had to figure out what "swag" was. And that made me feel old because now there are colloquialisms used by the youths around me that I don't understand. That's the definition of Old Person. To make it worse my very first thought when I heard the word swag was, "That's a dumb word. What's wrong with these kids?" Old! I'm old now. Old and lame and judgemental. Bring on the Best of Michael Bolton!

Once I did figure out the general edges of what swag was, and no I'm not wasting any time in my book explaining it because I'm a grumpy old man now, I had to get a hat. A swaggy hat. It's hard to shop for something when you aren't sure what it is you're looking for. The hat I settled on after much debate and Googling was roundly agreed to be swaggerific at school the next day by my class, so I guess I chose wisely. Swag Day also meant I got to rock a tie, vest, and pocket watch. I do love wearing my vest and pocket watch. Swag Day isn't so bad. Still a dumb name though.

Pajama Day is a great day too. To understand the allure of Pajama Day you must first realize that wearing nice clothes every day can be a drag, and getting comfortable is a nice pick-me-up. Imagine if your boss walked into your office and gave you permission to not get dressed for work tomorrow. If you're my kind of people then you're all over that like white on rice on a paper plate in a snowstorm.

The Powers That Be are always very specific when sending home the note about Pajama Day. "Must be SCHOOL APPROPRIATE." Thou shalt not wear your shorty short shorts, older girl children. No one wants to see that. I struggled with what to wear on Pajama Day at first for reasons you don't need to know about but can probably infer, so my wife got to go to her most favorite place in the word- Target. Target has a great selection of pajamas and I went home with a brand new pair of Darth Vader pj pants and a comfy shirt. Wearing Vader pj pants to school is a test. Any child who doesn't know who the guy on Mr. Robertson's pajamas is gets a stern note home chastising his or her parents. Really, your kid got all the way to fourth grade without learning about Star Wars? I question your parenting, sir and madam.

Sports Day means I get to wear a football jersey my dad bought me, or a triathlon race shirt. Still beats a button-up. And I get to argue with the child who wears a San Francisco Giants shirt to school. Get out of my classroom. Boo Giants.Go Dodgers.

I don't play during Twin Day because, as I tell my students, "I don't have any friends." I love the kids who don't pay attention when I'm explaining the idea behind Twin Day, "dress up exactly like a friend." I always get the question, "What if you don't have a twin? I don't even have a brother." That doesn't get a real answer. That gets a Teacher Look.

My school used to do Nerd Day but dropped it because a) the term nerd isn't something we want to have our kids calling each other, b) nerd is commonly used as an insult but it means smart person, why would we want that connection made in a school, and c) some kids already dress stereotypically nerdy on their own without knowing it so it's mean and embarrassing to them. I've no problem with this. It isn't PC-Washing a fun day, it's increasing awareness about a potentially offensive situation.

We've tried Famous Literary Character Day but that's hard to do. I think we got a lot of Harrys and Hermiones that year. Wizards are easy, all you need is a cloak. Thing 1 and Thing 2 popped up. The kids should have dressed as superheroes. Comic books are literary. In my class, at least.

Some students get very into Spirit Week and participate to the hilt. Some don't care, and some half-way it. It's those two that concern me. The ones who act like they don't care rarely don't actually care. What they care about is not looking foolish. That's one of the reasons I dress up. Too Cool Disease is rampant and sad. No child should be Too Cool for something as fun as Pajama Day or Sports Day. I encourage my class to not be afraid to look silly in everything else we do, why would Spirit Days be any different?

Read Across America, Dr. Seuss's birthday, always has me in a yellow t-shirt with an iron-on blue star on the tummy. Maybe a wild yellow wig if I can find it in my closet. Why a Star Bellied Sneetch? Because they are the best Sneetches on the beaches, of course! It also means I get to read the book to my kids and they get to argue with me about how I'm wrong about the Star-Bellies being the best. I trick them into learning. Prove to me I'm wrong using examples from the story.

There is another day where dressing up is encouraged, at least in some schools. I've heard some have stopped allowing dressing up on this the most important of holidays but I refuse to believe it. It can't be true. No one could be that uptight and lame. The best day to dress up at school is...Halloween!

I adore Halloween. It is by far my favorite holiday. When my students ask why, I tell them it's because it's the one day of the year I'm allowed and encouraged to scare children outside of the classroom. Really it's because I'm a grown man who embraces excuses to wear a costume. If today I can be Batman then today I *am* Batman.

When I was in school we used to have Halloween parades around campus. Everyone dressed up and we would go trooping around the quad, strutting our stuff, showing off the cool costume we'd had planned out since last year (or forced mom to panic buy last night). You brought a change of clothes in your bag and you enjoyed the day. It isn't often you get to sit in class with a stitched up hockey player, a zombie, a werewolf, Wonder Woman, and a fairy.

Now many of my students don't dress up and we don't have a parade. If I were a principal we would, but for now parades Disrupt the Learning Environment. We have lots of important things to be learning and nothing should interrupt that. Except multiple standardized tests.

I still dress up every year. One year I was in a particularly humorless grade level, and they were telling their students not to dress up at all. School is no place for fun, and it would be distracting. The costumes would lead to widespread chaos and anarchy.

I disagreed. My class was well behaved every other day. I had no reason to believe that a few costumes would turn them into mindless anarchists. So I told them I was fine with their dressing up as long as they promised to behave like they always did. We made a deal. Students like deals. That year I was as gruesome a zombie as I thought administration would let me get away with. The Fun Police didn't say anything to me.

That is always the argument against dress up days- order will collapse and chaos will reign. That because the children are allowed to relax they will forget everything you've taught them. If you're a good teacher and you've trained your class well that simply isn't true. Clear expectations and a willingness to send a child to the office to get a change of clothes are all you need. Yes, there are rules. No masks that cover your face because I don't want anyone pulling a Dark Helmet to President Skroob on me. No weapons, I don't care how fake they look. A child cannot resist bouncing a foam sword off another child's head. I understand that. I swashbuckle around Target with one when I get bored. Or when I find one.

I hope Spirit Weeks and Halloween never go away.

Children need to see their school as a place where fun things can happen. I hope teachers will always dress up for these days. Children should see their teachers as more than just the sage on the stage, the serious woman standing before them wielding a math book. My kids got a day of instruction from Professor Severus Snape. We had a faux-potions lesson. I took ten points from Gryffindor.

And yes, one day I even dressed up as Clifford the Big Red Dog. It wasn't for a special dress up day. It was for some Student Parent Night. I volunteered because no one else would, because I can't say no, and because the child that lives in the back of my head shouted, "We've never worn one of those suits before! This'll be great!"

It was one of the big full-on costumes with the giant head that's impossible to see out of. I lost fifteen pounds in sweat that night. I ran over small people who don't know they exist below sight-lines. I scared other small people because Giant Walking Red Dog. But there is a parent at my school whose son still remembers me as the Guy in the Dog Costume. He's excited to someday be in my class because he thinks it will be fun.

He thinks school will be fun. That makes the long, hot, blind night as Clifford worth it.

Chapter 10: How You Talk When You Talk About Your Students

Fair warning- This is another Soapbox Chapter.

I firmly believe that when you say something, it etches a line in your brain. The more you say that thing, the deeper that etch becomes, until it is a groove, a crack, a crevasse.

This is why I can't stand teachers who constantly complain about their class.

I understand the occasional complaint. It is the right of every professional to have a bad day, come into the teachers' lounge, and blast away about this kid or that kid or your entire class for a minute. Sometimes you need that. It keeps you sane and keeps you from doing it in front of them.

My problem is with the teachers who do it everyday. Every day there is a child or group of children or their entire class who these teachers want to complain about. To them I have a few things to say.

The first is that if you're constantly complaining about a child, then the child is no longer at fault. You, as the teacher, are not doing enough to change their behavior. If the problem is always the same then my first question is- What are you doing about it? If you don't have a reasonable, flexible answer then you are actually the problem.

Now, I realize this sounds harsh. I know students who are hard to teach, who are hard to work with, who drive me up walls. But they are not broken and they are not bad kids. They are kids who make bad choices. They are frustrating, maddening, hair-tearing pains in the class. But they are not *bad*.

I've had students throw chairs at me, call me a person who fornicates with my mother, and kick me in the shins. I am not a saint. I would go home and rant about the behavior. Then I would struggle to find ways to reach them. The entire year would be a constant back and forth of making progress, whatever I did stops working, making progress, falling back, progress, regress. Tiny steps. Never letting myself become the problem. Never letting myself believe the child is wrong. Remembering he needed help that I couldn't find yet.

I know teachers who give up on students they feel they can't reach. "Well, soon the kid will be an x-grader, then she won't be my problem anymore."

You should be fired.

Today. Now. Soonest. You should find a job far far away from children.

That is why I'll never be an administrator.

Some teachers predict their students' future. Talking about how this kid will end up in prison, that kid is going to be pregnant before she gets out of high school, and oh boy, that kid is going to get beat up so much in middle school. You are no longer a teacher if you say those things about a student. Because your job, your Biggest, Most Important Job, is to do whatever you can to make those things not happen. If you're predicting those outcomes then you aren't doing your job. You're out loud admitting you aren't trying. Can you imagine what the parents would say if they heard you?

And don't blame it on the parents either. You know what? Sometimes, a lot of the time, yeah, these kids are kind of sideways because of the things the adults in their life put them through. There is literally nothing I can do about the past of some of my kids, as much as I wish I could. There is nothing I can do about what they go home to unless it forces me to be a mandated reporter.

But when they are with me I have All The Control. I have All The Responsibility. For the hours those kids are mine I will make them feel welcome and appreciated. Even the ones I sometimes want to pick up and shake. I will show them understanding and compassion and optimism because they need an adult to do that for them.

If you are a teacher, I ask that you think about what you say about your class to other people on a regular basis. I try extremely hard not to bad mouth any of my kids out loud. I will talk about student struggles, I'll be honest about kids who need help. But I will not trash them. I try to not even say things like, "Yeah, So-and-So is pretty dopey." I do say that sometimes, but not often. Because if you say it enough, even in jest, you start to believe it. You start to label your kids. You create those grooves in your brain. I do not understand teachers who don't seem to like their jobs or their students. Teachers who are years away from retirement counting down towards retirement? Leave the profession. Get a new job. I don't want to work with you. You obviously don't want to be here.

I realize how harsh all of this sounds. I've spent a lot of time in the company of these kinds of teachers. Teachers who are awful about their kids. Who say terribly mean things like they are jokes, except they are completely serious. I believe that every time you do that as a teacher you hurt your relationship with your class. I believe that students are smart enough to know, somewhere, that you feel that way about them.

To my kids' faces I say I don't like them. I scowl and growl and proclaim that schools would be better without children. I also tell them that I never smile, and that I never have smiled. I dislike smiles. Before they go to recess I remind them not to have fun. "There is no fun at school," I proclaim nearly every day. "School is a place for WORK. WORK is not FUN." And they know I don't mean a word of it. I know because I ask if they believe me and they laugh and say no.Which means I get to act shocked that they are calling their teacher a liar. Gasp and whatnot.

My goal is for my class to be the most positive room in

the school. I build relationships with my students so that they trust me with questions and problems. So that they feel safe. When people outside of my class ask me about my kids, yeah I have funny stories. Of course I do, children are hilarious. I also tell them how great my kids are.

The teacher influences the classroom in every possible way. I know teachers who, according to them, always have a room full of pains. A room full of children who just won't sit and learn like they *should*. Me? I always have a room full of weird kids. Every year I have 25 of the goofiest children I've ever seen.

The teacher influences the class. If you have a room full of kids, the entire class or nearly the entire class, who are giving you trouble, guess who the trouble actually is? I know exactly why I always have a strange group. I tell my students, "You are some of the weirdest children I've ever met. Why are you so weird?" They all know the answer without being told. "Our teacher is weird! We learn from the best!" I remind them that normal people are boring. Weird people make the more interesting friends.

If every year your class feels off, then it isn't the fault of the students in your class. This is a lesson in personal responsibility I drill into my student teachers. The buck stops with you. Thou Art The Teacher. Everything about your room, from the condition of the desks to the stuff on the walls to the test results to the overall class behavior reflects on you.

So when you talk about your kids, talk about them in a way that makes you happy to be around them. You will be spending 180 days with these people, and even more thinking about them. You are responsible for their growth as human beings, as citizens, as individuals for a year. When you speak about them show that you care. In your voice, in your words, in your actions. Even when you aren't with them. Because how you feel away from your class is how you feel in front of

them. And they can feel that.
steps off soapbox

Doug Robertson

Chapter 11: The Trunchbull and *Deep Breath* Parents

Question: What kind of a foolish teacher writes a chapter in his book about parents?

Answer: The kind who hopes to help parents.

Roald Dahl is my favorite children's author not named Dr. Seuss. *Matilda* is my favorite Roald Dahl book. My being a teacher and it being set in a school probably have something to do with that. Also, that the book is basically a love letter to reading and the value and intelligence of children.

Matilda contains my most favorite character in all of literature. She is more fun to read aloud than any single person ever put in print. She's brilliant. Before I start the book for my class (*Matilda* is always the first read aloud of the year) I tell them my most favorite character lives in this book and I make them guess who it is. They always guess Ms. Honey. Ms. Honey is a wonderful person and an excellent example of a caring, lovely teacher children in the bottom form, and all forms, need. But she's not my favorite.

I love The Trunchbull.

Ms. Agatha Trunchbull, Headmistress of Crunchem Hall, is without a doubt the most fun character ever written for a teacher to read to his class. She never speaks, she only barks and shouts. There are Trunchbull chapters that nearly make me hoarse. She says wonderfully evil things that must make the people passing by my classroom think I'm the most awful person on the planet. "You ignorant little slug! You witless weed! You empty-headed hamster! You stupid glob of glue!"

She dangles small children by their ears and throws a girl over the fence by her pigtails. She goes to 11. I quote her for the rest of the year, telling my students how wonderful a school would be without children. "It's no good *telling* them, Ms. Honey. You've got to *hammer* it into them." Introducing the Trunchbull early in the year sets the tone for the rest of the year. The students know I think she's funny, and they know it's because she's ridiculous. I know they know because we talk about her. I can't assume they understand, every once in awhile you get a student who is immune to hyperbolic humor and needs to hear the explanation. Never assume they get the joke. Tell them the joke so they can be in on it. That way when I say Trunchbull things to them while we are out and about they laugh while nearby adults look horrified.

Roald Dahl understands and writes children with a depth of sympathy and understanding rarely seen in literature. Children are almost always the only people in his books that get treated well. Adults, not so much. At the start of *Matilda* he satires parents with laser-like precision bordering on the vicious. The first two paragraphs of the book are designed to delight teachers.

"It's a funny thing about mothers and fathers. Even when their own child is the most disgusting little blister you could ever imagine, they still think he or she is wonderful.
"Some parents go further. They become so blinded by adoration they manage to convince themselves their child has the qualities of genius."

Anyone who has sat through one day of parent conferences must stop after reading those words to collect themselves. Once the tears have dried and the teacher can see clearly, they are able to continue. From there he goes into a wonderful diatribe about the ways he would write report card comments, a section I think of at the end of every quarter. Who wouldn't like to have some fun with that? You can't, of course, but wouldn't it be nice? How creative could you be?

The reason those two paragraphs are so funny is the same reason anything is funny- They are based in truth. Parents love their children and think they are the best thing in the world. As they should. The problem happens when that interferes with the teacher doing her job.

Parents- I'm going to be straight up with you. Most teachers don't want to say this to you, but I will. I want you to know this isn't coming from a place of animosity or anger. The majority of my experiences with parents have been positive. Even those parents, though, sometimes need to hear what I'm about to say.

I am the professional here. This is my job. I've been well trained. I do it for a living. You need to trust me. I don't get paid based on your child's grades (yet). I don't get sick pleasure out of making your son cry. I'm not picking on your daughter via her report card. I'm not trying to ruin your weekend with my math homework. I really do believe the reading is more important than football practice. I could use help on this field trip, and your daughter would really dig it if you came. Yes, he does need all those folders and pencils and journals, they aren't that expensive at Target and you should see his desk without them. I really do know what is best in my classroom. The story your son is telling you about what happened at recess might be true-ish, I'm not saying he's lying, but he might be conveniently forgetting context. I would very much appreciate it if you ask me my version of something before you get angry with me. I write notes home so you know what is going on, please write me back so I know you saw the note. And please please please don't call my classroom in the middle of the day. I'm busy.

These are not the gripes of a teacher burned by parents. These aren't directed at specific people. These are simply the guidelines I would give to any parent.

As a teacher, I ask that you trust my judgement. I am fair. If your daughter got in trouble in class, the odds that she deserved to get in trouble are 100%, no matter what she tells

81

you. I have no problem with you coming to me and asking me about it. Please do! I do take issue with you complaining to her about her teacher, or going over me straight to my principal. He's got better things to do. Ask me first. If you don't like my answer, then I'll walk you to his office and wait with you outside his door. Complaining to her about her teacher only serves to undermine the work I've done with her. Please don't break me down. That makes my job harder.

I send a lot of paperwork home. I know I do. Especially at the beginning of the year. Oy, the beginning of the year stack o' papers is taller than some kindergarteners I know. I realize you hate reading through all of that. Trust me, I hate reading through all of it too. But I would not send it home if it wasn't important. Making copies is not my idea of a good time. I beg that you wade through it all and keep it somewhere for the duration of the year, returning signed to me what I need signed.

I send home my homework policy. When you ask me why they have homework all the time, I secretly wonder why you don't already know that. When you bring in cupcakes in the middle of the day because it's Sean's birthday I wish that you had read the paper detailing how we handle birthdays in my class. (Bring treats, but in the last five minutes. I won't hand them out before that. I'll put them in the back. Where they will probably get eaten by ants. Sorry, but I warned you.) My discipline plan is very clear, and I send it home so I know you know why things happen in class. You need to know that if your child is calling you at work someone's apple cart had gotten very upset during the day. I send the homework journal home filled out every night. Please read it. Actually read it. Don't just sign it. Look at it. See if what they wrote makes sense to you. It helps all of us- you, me, and your child.

Speaking of homework, I realize homework on the weekend and over break is a huge bummer. I do. I don't want to give it. Sometimes I have to. Sometimes there is so much to get done that work spills over. I'm not trying to ruin your break. I'm not giving that much. If it's a Big Project like a book report or a science project I have given your child (and you through the paper I sent home detailing the project, the homework planner, and the online homework planner) ample warning that it was coming. Proper planning would prevent overwhelming break homework. Normally all I'm assigning is some reading anyway. They should be doing that on their own.

Side Note: Please have a library card. Libraries are awesome. And free. Best deal in town.

All teachers have Parent Stories. I've only ever dealt with a few unreasonable mothers and fathers. One cornered me in the parking lot after school and declared at the top of her lungs that I was NOT to give her daughter homework over the weekend and if I dared to I would NOT punish her for not turning it in. Please don't tell me how to grade their work. And don't tell me what I'm NOT going to do. I have a hard enough time NOT being flip to adults as it is.

The complaint I get that confuses me the most, and I rarely hear it but every teacher does, is when a parent tells me I'm mean to her child.

I'm not.

Sorry, but you're wrong. Outright, without a doubt, incorrect. I am not mean to your child. I am not a Mean Teacher. You've got to believe me. I am just about as far away from a Mean Teacher as a person can get. I've worked with Mean Teachers and that cured me of any malice which may have hidden in my heart when it comes to students. If anything I fall the other way. I'm much too nice of a teacher most of the time. My discipline philosophy allows me to be. I want to enjoy school. It's where I spend most of my time. I want your child to enjoy school for the same reason. I'm not mean. Please ask your child for more details. Please filter those details not through your Parent Brain, but through your Adult Brain.

I'm sure you can guess what my biggest complaint about parents probably is. I would guess it's the same as most teachers. Some of you- no, not you the reader, you're awesome- some of them, then, aren't involved enough. I am not at your kitchen table while my student is doing their homework. I need someone else to be. We are working together here. I never send home work that I don't think your child can do. Homework is review and practice, that's all it is. They *know* how to do it. If they don't, the book they brought home explains it. The journal has notes that explain it. The top of the page has directions. But you might need to help. Don't tell them the answer, guide them to it. Check in with what they are reading. Question me about their report card. Please. It keeps me honest, provided you do it respectfully and not, "My son is NOT Well Below in math! He's excellent at math at home! He taught his baby sister and the neighbor's dog how to multiply seven digit numbers in their heads!" That doesn't help our discussion and it certainly doesn't help the student.

I understand circumstances prevent some parents from being involved. I know you might be a single mom working two jobs who never gets to see her children because you leave before they catch the bus and get home in time for dinner and bed. I'm asking that you take whatever time you have and ask your daughter to read to you for a few minutes before she goes to sleep. You have no idea how helpful that is for her. Reading aloud helps children hear the words, which helps comprehension. It helps you assess where they are because you'll be able to hear where she struggles and whether or not she reads with expression. Reading with expression means she is comprehending as she reads, and that's wonderful because then you know she isn't spending time decoding the words.

You'll better understand why that grade is what it is.

Time in the car can be used for slipping some education on them. I don't understand televisions in the car. Maybe that makes me old and lame, and that's fine. But the car is one place where you have uninterrupted conversation time with your child. Quiz them on their times tables. Not the whole trip, no one wants to spend thirty minutes doing mental multiplication, so maybe just at red lights. If they aren't into it make it a game, go back and forth. The child gets to ask you a times table question, then you get to ask one back. You still get to find out how well your son knows multiplication because if he asks you 4 x 4 and you say 17 and he doesn't say anything, you know he's not solid on that skill.

Reading isn't the only time children practice comprehension. When they watch TV, play video games, or go to a movie they are thinking about a story. Ask questions during commercials. Where are they? Who is the main character? What is happening? When does this take place? And the Most Important Question- WHY? Why did that happen? Why does that character feel that way? If it's a video game, Why did you have to do that?

"Why" makes a brain explain more than any other question. It is my favorite question. It works for any subject. Why did the Trunchbull call everyone into the auditorium? Why is 5 x 4 = 20? Why do you think it might rain today? Why did you like that movie? Drive your child crazy with questions! Encourage them to ask you questions!

Oh! That's a scary thing, isn't it? What if they ask you a question you don't know the answer to? New teachers have this same fear. I'm supposed to be the smartest one in the room. I'm the Teacher. I'm the Parent. I'm the Adult. I should have all the answers.

No. No, you shouldn't. Be wrong. Be unsure. That tells your child that being wrong is okay. I tell my students weekly that I want them to get things wrong. My job is to teach them, but if they know everything I have nothing *to* teach them. Them being wrong keeps me employed. I will never ever yell at someone for being wrong. I'll get on their case for not trying, that's a huge problem, but being wrong? Nope. Be wrong. Humans are wrong with startling regularity. You can't learn unless you're wrong first. I tell my kids I'm wrong all the time. When I make a mistake in class they point it out. Oh, there is nothing more fun than pointing out your teacher's mistake. "Mr. Robertson! The answer is 52! You wrote 55!" "Why so I did. Thank you." "Mr. Robertson, you misspelled ceiling! Again." Ceiling, for those of you who don't know, is one of the most frustrating words in the English language. It never looks right.

Being wrong is learning.

The best part of telling your child that you don't know is it means you get to *learn something together*! We now live in a world where all the knowledge is quite literally at our fingertips. The Google Knows All. Take advantage of your smart phone. Show your child how you find out something when you don't know. Show him how to comb through the bad information to find the good. He will get to learn from you. If you're brave enough to be wrong, your son will come to my class and he'll be brave enough to be wrong.

Be involved in the classroom. I need chaperones for field trips. There are always a few parents who leap at the chance, waving their hands and calling, "Me! Me! Oh oh oh, Mr. Kotter! Pick me!" They are great, wonderful, fantastic. But I don't just want them. Take a sick day and come along. Please. I promise you'll enjoy it, save for maybe the bus ride. I hate the bus. Always feel car sick on the bus. The teacher can't get car sick! Yes, he can, he just can't complain about it. He also can't beg the bus driver to stop because he needs to pee and didn't get a chance before he left the museum because he was busy herding children. He also secretly likes it when the kids sing on the bus. It feels right. Come experience that.

One of my favorite teaching movies is Kindergarten Cop. It's hilarious. Arnold is at the top of his comedy game. The kids are great. His classroom is bigger than some cafeterias, but whatever, it's a movie.

My favorite part of that movie is when Arnold threatens to beat the daylights out of the abusive father. We can't do that, obviously. We can do some things, we have to report, but these are my kids too. Reporting doesn't feel like enough. I've had enough hard students to know that many are that way because of something a parent has done. I've had the Kindergarten Cop Fantasy many times. I've had kids where I stopped digging into their past because it made me sick. I don't have to tell you not to be that parent. I will tell you that we know when you are. And your child is much more important to me than your freedom is.

Parents and teachers should form a partnership. I appreciate how hard your job is. I ask that you appreciate how hard mine is. I've had wonderful, amazing parents over the years. Parents I became friends with after their daughter left my class. We don't have to go that far, but mutual respect would be nice. My goal is the same as your goal- To make your child the best human he or she can be. We might have different ways of going about it. We might have different views of what that means. We still need to come together for him. Work with me here. Please.

Doug Robertson

Chapter 12: Bodily Functions

The cliche is that children are walking germ factories.

The truth is so much more icky.

Children are not walking germ factories because of any personal failing on their part. Children are walking germ factories because children get into everything. Touch touch touch. Fall and touch. Lick and touch. Sneeze and touch. Pick and touch. Touch touch touch.

The smaller they are, the grosser they can be. Small children are constantly leaking. Bodily fluids ooze out of orifices at a rate that would incapacitate a grown man. I've known tiny humans whose noses ran for years at a time. Every inhalation doubled as a sniffle. When I was small I had allergies and the collar of my shirt became a convenient wipe. I've since learned that I was not the first to figure this out, nor will I be the last. If your shirt isn't supposed to be a tissue it shouldn't be so soft and right there up by your nose. We should make shirt collars out of some type of sandpaper. You'd be able to tell the kindergarteners with hay fever by counting the ones with a nub instead of a nose.

I keep boxes of tissue all over my classroom. Four at least. One by my desk in the front of the room since I never really grew out of sneezing because of dust or dander or sunlight. One on every other wall. Students are never more than a few feet from a box of tissues. This doesn't stop the child sitting on the far right from getting a wipe from the box on the far left via the most circuitous route possible, but at least the option is there.

The standing rule in my classroom is that you cannot get out of your seat for any reason while I'm teaching. I say that to my students at the beginning of every year. It is part of the First Day Spiel. Thou shalt stay in thy seat. I immediately follow this up with caveats. The first is UNLESS you have sneezed all over yourself. Children do this all the time because most children sneeze disproportionately to their size. The smallest child in class will knock over a stack of books with a sneeze. She will rattle windows and wake babies in nearby houses.

It is never, ever, a dry sneeze either. How I yearn for dry sneezes. During cold season I sometimes wish the parents of my students would point their blow dryer right up their son's nasal cavity before getting in the car in the morning. Dry that bad boy right out. A bloody nose is a hundred times less disgusting than snot. Snot has weight and mass. Snot is the stickiest natural substance known to man. Ancient man used to use mammoth snot to caulk the roofs of their huts in the rainy season. I've seen kindergarteners become conjoined twins because they sneezed on each other at the same time.

Thus the first exception to my rule. You have to tell children this exception too, especially the good kids. A good kid will explode, cover her face, and stare at you with horror in her eyes. A good strong sneeze acts like a hard restart in your brain, like dropping your cell phone and the battery popping out. The brain needs a moment to reboot. If you haven't already input the code for automatic tissue retrieval and nose blowing the child will stare at you for minutes, waiting for someone to tell her what to do.

Snot is horrifying, even your own. George Carlin once said you would wipe it on a flaming piece of wood if you had to, just to get it off you. I make sure they know to get up and blow their nose, clean themselves up. Wash your hands. With soap, Christopher. Sometimes it's a worst-case sneeze and the child also has to wipe his desk, get a new paper, clean his pencil, wash his neighbor's hair (just cut it, that stuff is never coming out), and mop the floor. Science help you if you've got carpet instead of tile in your class. Might as well junk the whole room and start over. It's only a matter of time before someone steps on it and gets stuck there forever.

The other caveat to Thou Shalt Stay In Thy Seat is if you are about to be sick. Any kind of sick, I don't care what is about to come spraying out of you nor from what end, get out of my room. Go, run RUN to the bathroom. Even if you don't make it all the way there it is still better than doing it in the classroom.

Mostly, I'm talking about puke. Vomit. Spew. Throw up. Sick. Some children throw up more often than frat boys convinced they are living it up. The trick is getting that moment of warning before it happens. They know it is about to happen. The Vomit Voice speaks to all. But how much time to do you have? How far are they from the door? Some students feel it coming far enough in advance. "Mr. Robertson...I don't feel good..." A child about to lose it has a look. A pale, sickly pallor. An experienced teacher has seen it before.

"Go. Go to the bathroom. Gogogo!"

This might seem harsh. Maybe you think I should ask very nicely what is wrong and what they had to eat. Nope, now is not the time for that. Vesuvius is bubbling and you don't know when it is going to blow. Urgency supersedes a fare-thee-well. Yes, throwing up will probably ruin that student's day. But throwing up in the room will ruin the entire class's day. That is a smell that does not come out. Sympathetic puking becomes a real concern. Not just for the students either. I'm okay around a lot of fluids, but those smells...I struggle to keep it together. I'm not above taking a class outside for the day. You do your best not to embarrass the sick child, of course. I remind the class that this happens, that sometimes people get sick, and I praise the ill one for getting out of the classroom in time. Even if they only make it to the grass outside the room that is still better than doing it in class.

91

May you never experience a bus sick child. Trapped in a warm, enclosed can... *bjork*

There might be much less warning. It can hit a body all at once, with barely any notice at all. Not even a, "How do you do." I once watched a little girl go from normal to pale in two seconds. Poor thing had time to look at me with frightened eyes that communicated everything. I started pointing at the door as she started to speak, "Mr. Robertson, I bleeeeehhhh!!!!" All over her desk. So helpless. Nothing I could do. She cried. Of course she cried, it's one of the most embarrassing things that can happen in class. Not THE most, we're getting there, but in the top two.

This is a situation your teacher classes in college don't prepare you for. You are now comforting a sick, mortified kid while getting her out of the room to the nurse while keeping the other 24 from freaking out and/or following suit, especially the kid next to the sick one. If you've done the proper groundwork and your class is well behaved this isn't too bad, they know what is expected of them even in unusual situations. Get the child to the nurse, keep the class calm, call the office for clean up, don't touch it yourself, and find a reason to work outside for the next twenty minutes. Don't look at it or smell it. I've never thrown up in front of my class and I hope I never will, but that would do it.

Never, ever, touch anything that comes out of a child. Teachers do not get paid enough. Everyone is health-aware enough now that we should all have gloves in our classrooms, so if you absolutely have to make contact, say for a bleeder, you have protection. But puke? Nope. Not going near it. Only my own child's. Most bleeders are things students can handle on their own anyway. A bloody nose should be taken care of calmly, quickly, and smoothly. Fingers pinch the bridge of the nose, tilt your head down or keep it neutral, grab a handful of tissues, go to the bathroom or nurse until it stops. There isn't anything else you can do about it. The child can do all of that on their own. Unless they are tiny. Another reason kindergarten teachers are saints.

The worst though, the absolute worst, is *accidents*. By fourth grade the incidence of *accidents* is greatly reduced. It rarely happens. Smaller kids it happens more to. Kinder I don't want to think about. Kinder and pre-k classes make the kids leave a change of clothes in their cubbies just in case of *accidents* they happen so much. Still though, even with bigger kids it can happen. It will probably happen. I don't know how.

An accident almost always happens quietly. You don't know what is going on until the smell hits you. What *is* that smell? No, no it couldn't be. But it smells like- No. No no no no. Awww, man. Really?

Again, I don't want to put my student into therapy. I don't want to destroy the rest of his year. But I have to deal with it. Sometimes the child raises his hand. I had a kid once do it almost proudly, "Mr. Robertson, I just peed." What? Why? Go away. Now. Take your chair with you. Yes, take your chair with you. Trust me, you don't want the chair in your room. Chairs are concave. That means chairs are built to form puddles. Get it out of here.

Sometimes they are so ashamed they try to hide it. The child will pretend nothing is wrong. Like maybe they are the only one that smells it. A well trained class, a respectful class, will still react. Either the kid next to the wet child will prod him until he tells you, or the neighbor will report him herself.

Number Two, real accidents, I wish never happened at all. In fourth grade it is very rare. Even in third. I assume kindergarten is when this problem is the most serious. Again, that doesn't mean it doesn't happen, but when it does it is more the sudden illness type. We've all had that. You're sitting around and suddenly you brain shouts, "DANGER! EMERGENCY EVACUATION IN 10...9...8..." It happens to children too. Much like the child about to throw up you can see it on their face. The boy is working along and then sudden panic strikes. Flop sweat, wide eyes, you can almost hear the countdown. If you're on top of it you're telling him to run as he is raising his hand.

Standing rule in my room for these kinds of sudden illness is don't even ask, just go. Just go go go. I will never yell at you for taking care of yourself. That's not disrespectful. Hopefully they make it in time. Hopefully I can get the office ladies to make that follow-up phone call to the parent. I don't want to.

The important thing to remember in all of this is it might be the Worst Thing to happen to the child that year, possibly ever, in school. A good teacher has sympathy for that. Even if we are grossed out. If you can't believe the child let that happen to himself, you need to understand that he probably didn't. Who wants to explode or leak in front of their peers? No one.

I address it immediately, telling my class it happens and we need to be understanding. There will be No Teasing or the world will fall down upon the teaser's shoulders. These kinds of things happen to adults too, as much as we don't want to admit it or talk about it. Empathizing with your students is always paramount. Empathy will help them get over the embarrassment. Empathy will build and strengthen the bond in your classroom.

It's gross. It's icky. Humans are gross and icky. Sometimes we have to pretend to be adults and act like it doesn't bother us.

Then, when you're alone, dry heave and do the Icky Yucky Gross Dance. You know it- up on your toes, shaking your hands and shoulders, getitoffame!

Blech.

Chapter 13: Indoor Recess is Evil

I treasure recess time.

Recess time is my time. My time to copy or pee or rest my head on my desk for a few minutes.

Recess time is my students' time. Their time to run and scream and play and get all of that energy out of their systems.

Indoor recess is a terrible thing. When black clouds roll over my school I stand outside shaking my fist at the sky. My kids quickly learn that I strongly dislike the idea that they will not have recess. Recess is their right. It is my right. I curse the gods for taking that right away from me.

Sometimes I curse administration for it too. I don't know who makes the call for indoor recess. I know it is someone's job to look outside and say, "Welp, we can't send children outside in this. Ring the bells!" Then a complicated series of levers and pulleys is activated in a Rube Goldbergesque fashion, culminating in those terrible three bells ringing out across the campus. At which point I look up from my vocabulary lesson and snarl at the ceiling.

I admit it, as soon as the indoor recess bell rings I go outside. I check up on whomever makes the decision that students absolutely cannot go out and play today. I do not trust that person. My opinion of Unplayable and theirs does not often match. Misting is not raining. Mist will not ruin clothes, it will not soak the children, it will not make them slip and fall and die. Misting is not a reason to keep them inside. Puddles are not a reason to keep them inside. If it was raining but has since stopped take them out! Maybe the first recess had to be canceled but since then the situation has changed, and with it should change the status of recess. Let my people go.

Don't tell me the puddles present a danger or an issue because what if a student falls into one? My students will not fall into one, or slip into one, or play in one. Why do I know that for certain? Because I've told them many times that puddles are not for playing. I've told them they will get into trouble for playing in the puddles. It's blue sky clear. If it isn't raining we will go outside.

That's often a small gamble on my part, especially if the rainy day bell has been rung. It's overcast, but not raining. I tell my students before we go out if it starts to rain, and I mean actual drops falling on my head in a regular manner, not a couple of sprinkles, we will immediately form up and head back to class. If they can't handle that we won't do it again. Every once in a great while I'll get all the way to the basketball courts only to have to turn around after two minutes. Those few times are worth all of the times that I'm smarter than the clouds and my kids get a full and complete 20 minutes of energy expenditure. A little damp never hurt anyone. I've been heard to grumble under my breath, "There are children going to recess in the snow on the East coast and we are scared of a few puddles."

There are times when indoor recess is unavoidable. The rain keeps coming down. There's hurricanes a-blowin'. The water's five feet high and rising. I have to keep the class inside. What a bummer.

We play games during indoor recess. We have to. Eventually I get the class trained enough to run the games on their own. This isn't because I don't want to talk to them, but because as third or fourth graders they are old enough to follow a simple set of rules and be lead by a peer. Here are a few of my favorite indoor recess time-passers:

Four Corners- Four Corners is a classic skating rink game. I number each corner of my room 1, 2, 3 and 4 and choose an It. The It comes up to the front and faces the board. We are cued to specific words. If a student moves before the magic words are spoken they forfeit their opportunity and have to sit down.

"Mix 'em up," the It calls. Everyone interested in playing quickly walks (Walks! WALKS!) to the corner of their choosing while the It counts backwards from ten. Ten seconds is more than enough time. The It then picks a number and the students standing at that number sit back in their seats and are out. Repeat, repeat, rinse, and repeat until there are only four children left. The number the It says in the last round is the winner and the new It.

Things to watch out for- The It almost never repeats the same number twice in a row. It doesn't take long for the class to figure that out. They will bunch at the number the It just called. That works for one round. Then, hopefully, the next the It sees that and nails 3/4 of the class immediately. Also, I tell them I don't want an empty corner. If the It calls an empty corner the It wins and gets to start all over. No one likes it when the It wins. Feels unnatural. Like kissing your sister, or a football game ending with a tie.

Hangman- Everyone knows Hangman. It is not a complicated game. The difficulty of Hangman depends on how sadistic you are to your class. Are you a feet, legs, body, arms, head, dead teacher? Or are you a feet, legs, body, arms, hands, fingers, head, eyes, nose, mouth, hair, ears, please win, really why are you guessing z again, come on guys a vowel please, fine he's dead teacher? That is pretty much the only way to mix the game up.

My biggest problem playing Hangman is I'm not a great speller in my head. I have to write the word down and see it to be able to spell it. I'm visual like that. Many students also aren't great mental spellers. I make them write the word down before putting up the dashes. Otherwise we end up with three extra blank spots or the child standing in front of their blanks spelling it out out loud so everyone in the front row can hear her trying to figure out where the f goes.

I'm a Hangman with a face teacher. No hair or ears, but

you get to see his sad, sad face before he dies.

Around the World- Around the World is either a great game that a child loves or a terrible game that a child hates. There is very little in-between.

Around the World is a multiplication speed test. Two students face-off against one another and I give them a simple one digit by one digit multiplication problem. The first person to say the correct answer wins and moves on. The loser sits back down. If you're good at times tables you'll do well. If you're struggling with times tables you're going to lose. I try to use this as motivation for those who aren't great with their multiplication. Very quickly the class knows who is going to do well. They know who is blazing quick with 7x8 (the hardest single digit multiplication problem). I turn it into that child vs. The World. There is no taunting or teasing, but they can cheer their friends on. Upsets are great, and I allow my class to react like they're watching a sporting event. Within reason, of course. It is a lot of fun when the unexpected child beats the kid everyone expects to do a full lap.

I'm also pretty serious about effort in Around the World. If the child isn't going to try I don't let him or her play this game or the next. There is nothing lost in putting forth an effort. Sometimes I talk to the kids I know do well before we play and ask them not to throw the game, but to slow themselves down a second or two. Help their fellow classmates succeed. That's not a participation trophy mentality. That's students helping students.

Heads-Up Seven-Up- Heads-up Seven-Up is a game you completely forgot about until right this second unless you are currently teaching. Suddenly memories of Heads-Up Seven-Up are flooding back. It is the simplest of classroom games. You choose five or six or seven (traditionally it's seven, hence the name, but that doesn't work in smaller classes) children to come to the front of the room. They say, "Heads down, thumbs up!" You turn off the lights and the chosen children quietly make their way around the room touching one thumb of a classmate and reforming in the front. When everyone has touched a thumb they pronounce, "Heads-up Seven-up!" and you turn on the lights. Students blink, dazed by the dark-to-light transition, and if their thumb was touched they stand up to guess who picked them.

Strategy abounds for Head-Up Seven-Up. If you're a picker then you tip-toe so no one recognizes your footsteps. Students believe everyone becomes bats in the dark, and their super-sensitive hearing allows them to identify classmates by footfall. You also vary the way which you press down thumbs. Some push hard, to be sure the person knows they've been picked. Some barely brush the thumb. That's the worst, then they stand there for a half hour breathing on someone's thumb until that person registers that something is touching them. I don't know if you can tell who's thumb it is by intensity of touch, but I do know I believed my classmates could when I was small.

If you're one of the ones with your head down you are furiously concentrating on footfall and thumb texture and pressure. You might also be sneaky. Sneaky children hang their noses off the edge of the desk hoping to catch a glimpse of shoes. Sneaky children get caught by the teacher who knows all the tricks. Sneaky children are rarely as sneaky as they think they are.

The best part of Heads-Up Seven-Up is when the pickers get wiped clean by those they picked (this sentence sounds like it belongs in the Bodily Functions chapter, doesn't it?). For each successive child the odds go up of choosing the correct person. If the first six guess right that seventh kid does a happy dance before triumphantly pointing out their foe.

Hopefully.

Sparkle- Sparkle is a spelling game. I much enjoy Sparkle

as a way to practice spelling words. In Sparkle everyone stands and I describe a path through the class. It needs to be a simple path, around one group, straight to the next group, and so forth. If you're a Rows Teacher then up one row, back the next. To play Sparkle I say a spelling word. The student who has been chosen to start says the first letter of that word. The next child says the next letter, and so on. Um, Uh, and Er are not letters. If you say um, uh, or er you have to sit down. If the person in front of you sits down you have to say their letter. This means that the class has to be quiet so everyone knows what the last correct letter said was. There are times when a line of students aren't paying attention and four or five will fall in a row because one person got a letter wrong and those behind him weren't paying attention. The word ends not with the last letter, but with the person after the last letter saying, "Sparkle." That shows they know the word is over. I don't know why Sparkle is the word that means The End. I stole the game from somewhere and I like the idea of making some of the tough kids happily exclaim, "Sparkle!"

I go through the spelling list until everyone but one student is eliminated. Often I'll get down to two or three people who refuse to make a mistake. That's when vocabulary words come in. And speed. Speed is key. Back and forth, no hesitation in the letter-calling. Watching the class watch two children duel is like watching a Wimbledon crowd on fast forward. If I think they are evenly matched (*read*: the bell is about to ring) I'll call it and declare a tie.

Connect Four- I don't explain Connect Four. To introduce it I say, "We are going to play a game. I'm not going to tell you the rules. I'm going to beat you at the game."

Using the overhead I display a grid with the x and y axis labeled. I call out a pair of coordinates, and put a point on those coordinates. I don't tell them I'm calling coordinates, and the first time we play the game we probably haven't gone over graphing yet. After I go the first child has to tell me two numbers and I place a point wherever they said to, as long as it's on the graph. All the clues for how the game works are there from the first move, but it takes a few games for them to figure it out.

I beat the class in four moves three or four times. I don't let them talk to each other so everyone has to puzzle it out by themselves. Three kids in a row might figure it out and build a line- 2, 3; 3, 3; 4, 3. But then the fourth kid still doesn't understand and veers wildly off the reservation with 7, 8. Once enough of the class has figured it out I split them in half and play them against each other. Every once in awhile I'll let them challenge me. One person can pretty much always beat a group. One-on-one it's harder because one person can plan ahead. So I cheat by never playing one-on-one. I'm allowed to cheat. I'm the teacher.

By the time we're done playing I've taught my entire class coordinate graphing through a game they've enjoyed. They didn't even realize they were learning a standard.

As Bugs would say, "Ain't I a stinker?"

Doug Robertson

Chapter 14: The "E" Word

Let's get this out of the way right now- Everyone curses. Even if you don't do it out loud, you still curse. Even Mother Theresa dropped an internal f-bomb or two when she let a bowl of soup slip on her way to feeding another hungry soul. Words exist for a reason, and some words evolved for very specific usages. I'm not going to get into that. You want to read about the best ways to curse, go buy a George Carlin book. After you finish this one. Please.

I hope parents know teachers don't curse at students. We don't. Not with our outside voices at least. But, just like you we do get frustrated. When we get frustrated we talk to ourselves. Right now I imagine there are some parents and teachers shaking their heads at me, "No, you fool! Don't say that! Teachers are all wonderful people who never ever have a negative thought about children ever!"

Yeah, no. Good teachers don't indulge the negative thoughts. We don't dwell on negative thoughts. But humans have negative thoughts. We have the vocabulary to express those thoughts. Once you know a word your brain automatically finds ways to use it. That's why I push learning vocabulary words so hard. I forbid words like "very" and "really" and "good" and "bad" because they are boring and the kids can do better. Those words aren't good, in fact they are really very bad. More words mean more options for clearly expressing yourself, and a greater ease of doing so. So we do. On the inside.

However, parents- your kids know those words too. They might not know exactly what they mean, but they know context. They know about where the word should go. Listening to a child curse can be hilarious. Listening to a child *think* he is cursing is even better.

My wife is also a teacher and for a while she taught pre-k.

These are the tiniest humans at a school. They are three to four years old. One of her students wasn't too vocal, most three year olds aren't and special education students especially, but he sure thought he knew how to express his frustration. This small person would get fed up with whatever they were doing, look right at my wife or her EA, and spit, "Apple!" He would stomp around the room muttering to himself, "Apple! Apple. Apple." She has no proof he was cursing, or that he thought it was cursing. It's not really a conversation you have with a three year-old. I'm not sure that counts as a teachable moment.

"Now child, when you say apple, I think what you're trying to say is..."

principal dives into the room in slow motion, shouting, "Noooooooooo!" knocking you to the side

How a teacher deals with cursing in his or her classroom is a matter of personal preference living within school rules. I try very hard not to tweak on my students about most things. Bullying and outright disrespect will call down thunder and lightning, but other things, kid things, call for different types of reactions. You can't always slam your kids. If there are no levels to the jumping up and down they won't know when you're really being serious and when you're trying to correct a behavior.

Teaching the small people, as I do, I don't have to deal with too much cursing. Not in my classroom, and certainly not at me. I'm positive they curse down on the field or at home, where I can't hear them. I'm positive not because I'm thinking badly about my kids, but because I cursed when I was away from adults. Didn't you? Didn't almost everyone? I think often adults forget what it was like to be a child.

My job is to teach students to be respectful. Which means that using certain words as an interjection is not as bad as using them as an insult. Sometimes there are slips. Once a student noticed a mistake while we were correcting work one-on-one and muttered, "Sh*t." A good kid. Which means that immediately after he did it he realized what he'd said and he gave me the best wide-eyed Oh My God, I'm So Sorry face. I had two options- jump on him or not. I chose not to.

"Hey, do we talk like that in school?" "N-n-no..." "Ok, then I don't want to hear it again." And that's that. A minor mistake does not require detention. It requires gentle correction.

I also taught sixth grade, and kids that big do curse at each other in class, under their breath, trying to get away with it right in front of the teacher. They don't realize that a) I can see lips moving b) I remember being 12 and c) I can read their lips and/or hear. Students forget I also have ears. I use that to my advantage.

That's not to say I haven't had a student curse at me, about me, and regarding the things I may or may not have done with my mother. Because I have. Those students are dealt with differently. That is a child being disrespectful, hateful, and rude. That child goes to the office and does not collect $200.

Children cursing at each other carries the same weight in my class as children cursing at me. More, actually. I feel that being rude to peers should lead to a much tougher punishment than being rude to an adult. I'm still just punk rock enough to understand raging against authority. I'm not that old yet. But bullying a peer brings down stiff consequences. Bullying is a big thing in schools right now, and it should be. We need to get tougher on bullies, and better define bullying. I delve more into bullying in the next chapter.

Back to Apple, and kids like him. Misunderstanding and misuse of curse words is great. My day is full of serious moments and kids messing up adult vocabulary is a welcome change. What is even better is when they tattle about other kids cursing. I'm not a fan of tattling, and don't normally allow it. Once a child pre-tattled on himself. "Mr. Robertson, Andy is about to tell you that I pushed him down."

When a child tattles about cursing there is always the moment of hesitation. The child doesn't want to get in trouble for saying a Bad Word to a teacher, but they have to tell the teacher what the other student said. How do you approach that? The bold students come right out with it. "Kevin said 'f*ck!'" feeling safe in the knowledge that they aren't really the ones saying it, they are simply reporting it. Others beat around the bush with the "s-word" and the "f-word" and the "b-word". But which s-word do they mean? Some kids, and I'm ok with this, think "stupid" is a bad word. Which means that sometimes you get a trembling little girl standing beside you, "Mr. Robertson, Kevin said the s-word."

"Ok, sweetie, before I talk to him I need to know what he said. So you're not going to get in trouble, but please tell me the word. You can whisper it."

"Stupid."

Oh, ok. Calling someone stupid is mean and bullying. Not, however, what I was expecting.

Once this conversation did not go at all like I expected. It was near the end of the school year, and I was teaching third grade. A small girl child in my class came up to me at recess.

"Mr. Robertson," she said.

I leaned down, "Yes, child?"

"Mr. Robertson, Mark cursed at me." I know Mark. He's a trouble-maker. Story checks out so far.

"What did he say to you?"

She looks around nervously. She chews her bottom lip. "He called me the e-word."

Stop.

E-word? I being rapidly scanning my brain, looking for any possible e-word. I have a fairly wide and extensive foul word vocabulary and I don't think I have one e-word. I have to ask The Question and give The Permission.

"Sweetie, what is the e-word? You won't get in trouble, I promise."

She bites her lip. Her eyes dart around the field.

"Ugly."

Doug Robertson

Chapter 15: Bullying

It seems like everywhere you look today someone is talking about the Bullying Problem in today's schools. And for good reason. Bullying is a serious problem, and it requires serious solutions.

The reported instances of bullying have skyrocketed recently, but I don't think that's indicative of bullying actually increasing. Rather, the numbers are going up because more and more students are stepping forward and asking for help. We are better at defining bullying for ourselves and students, so we are better able to categorize abuse. Victim-shaming, telling the bullied to toughen up, is no longer acceptable. The divided climate of our culture has made it easier for students to feel safe reporting bullying, but it has also made it easier for bullies to find and attack targets.

In my classroom bullying carries the heaviest punishment. It is the worst behavior any teacher is likely to encounter on a regular basis. Sure, you might get cursing and disrespect and fighting, there could be some theft or insubordination, but more often than not those behaviors are directed at you, the teacher. I see a hard line between behaviors directed at me and behaviors directed at other students. I'm an adult, I have ways to deal with a child trying to wind me up. Their peers have no such toolkit and background. If a teacher takes the aggression of a student personally, that teacher needs to reevaluate why they are feeling that way. You are giving power to a child that a child should not have.

Cursing, disrespect, fighting, theft, insubordination can all be forms of bullying. Bullying is about power and the taking away of power. A bully is trying to make another person feel powerless, and by contrast make themselves feel powerful. A bully uses intimidation tactics to weaken their victim and make him or her feel unsafe. Nothing is more offensive in my classroom than someone making my students feel unsafe. I do not and will not stand for it. I will rarely yell at a student. Even when I'm boiling inside I breathe through that and do my best to keep it together. Catching a student bullying another student is one of the few things that make my grip slip. I have, I admit, shouted down a child for bullying. I try not to. I don't want to. I know it is not the proper way to handle a behavior. But my classroom should be a safe place. These children have been placed in my care and I will stand up for any one of them.

Students must be taught what bullying is, however. Like anything else, I cannot start punishing behaviors without first explaining what behaviors will lead to punishments. Too often adults assume children know what they should and shouldn't do and say. I can't assume the child's parents have talked to him about bullying. There's a scene in *Butch Cassidy and the Sundance Kid* where the titular pair is planning to escape a shoot-out by leaping into a river. Before they jump Sundance looks at Butch and says, "I can't swim!" Butch exclaims, "Why you crazy- The fall'll probably kill ya!" I don't want to be disciplining my students for something only to get the, "I can't swim!" look. I can't give them information that comes far too late, once we are already jumping.

We have a discussion early in the year, Week One, about bullying. Children don't know what bullying is, not really. They have an idea, but if you ask most kids to define bullying they'll say something along the lines of, "Someone being mean to you." This is technically correct, but only partially. Bullying is a behavior that happens repeatedly. Once is bad and should be corrected, but more than once is bullying. It is the repeated removal of power. "He called my shoes ugly," is not bullying. That's teasing, and should be dealt with, but isn't as serious. If he is constantly on your case about your shoes in a verbal, physical, or emotional way then he's bullying you.

I am loath to blame media for anything. I'm a product of video games, action movies, and heavy metal, and I am not a bully. However, the general tone of discourse in a lot of our culture is confrontational and overwrought. I have no problem with confrontation, if I have an issue with a person I will tell them. I don't have to get in their face about it, or be passive-aggressive about it though. There are ways to meet aggression without it degenerating into a fight. Right now it feels like the default setting for a discussion on television or the internet goes straight to saying the ugliest thing you can think of. I don't think my students watch those shows or go to those websites, but their parents do. Kids are sponges, and they are picking up behavior cues everywhere.

This, I'm sure, is a product of comment section culture. The anonymous world of the internet allows people to say horrible things all the time. Cyberbullying is a real thing. It might get scoffed at by old people who don't understand the interwebs, but kids take the internet seriously. We are now living in a time where the children in our classrooms don't know a world without internet. One only need spend a half hour surfing the web to find examples of the worst of human behavior perpetrated by some faceless nobody safe behind their computer screen, or by Ann Coulter. We might not take that seriously, but children do. That's their world now, and we as adults must teach them that even typing hurtful things is bullying, because words can hurt. The old rhyme about sticks and stones has never been true, but now that passing notes has been replaced by posting something on a worldwide public forum it has taken on a whole new level of wrong. Words can hurt you.

Children can be just as mean as adults, and yes they can be just as direct about it. Peer to peer interactions between children are more hurtful because they don't have the thick skin of experience that we have. Children rarely think in context or have an emotional buffer zone. Don't tell me that it is kids being kids. Don't tell me it toughens them up and gets them ready for the real world. Those are the excuses of past bullies trying to make their offenses seem like growth opportunities. "I wasn't being mean. I was helping him become a man! I'm telling you, Americans are being wussified by you people."

Bull. You don't become an adult by coping with hardship brought on by peers. I'm not a man because I got picked on in grade school, and you're not a man because you did the picking. Children need to be taught that abuse is never okay, and bullying is a form of abuse. I don't think this will create a nation of weak and wussified adults. It might create a nation of well-adjusted and balanced adults who are able to have a reasonable conversation, even with those they disagree with.

Part of my job is to be a defender of the weak. The thing we forget is all students are weak. They are children. They cannot yet defend themselves. Some children recognize their weakness, some have no idea. That doesn't matter. Teachers should defend everyone.

Soapbox Warning We still marginalize people in this country. Women are still fighting for equal rights decades after the suffrage movement. America still has a racial problem. The election of Barack Obama was met with celebration, but also with loud demands to see his birth certificate. No white president has ever been hounded by people who honestly believe he wasn't born in America. In this country we are still having debates on whether or not gay people should be allowed to get married. That's staggering and open marginalization. Bullying.

I teach lessons about segregation every year around Martin Luther King's birthday. Explaining white people and black people having different bathrooms to nine year olds is a lesson in how far we've come. If you could see the looks on my kids' faces you'd understand what I mean. "Wait, Mr. Robertson, I don't understand. Why couldn't they use the same water fountains? I mean, it's a water fountain." Serious, honest confusion. They don't get it. It isn't real to them. I guarantee that in less than fifteen years I will be teaching a whole new generation of children who will look at me exactly the same when we talk about the Second Civil Rights Movement in America. "My best friend has two dads. They're cool. Why couldn't they get married?" I will show them pictures of the protests happening in our country right this minute and they will look at the opposition side with the same lack of understanding that they look at the crowds of white people surrounding students entering the first integrated schools. I won't tell them how to feel, that isn't my job. I will tell them where we were and where we are and let them decide for themselves. *Places soapbox beneath desk*

I bring up gay marriage (aka a formalization of a loving relationship between two people) because the quickest way children are bullied is by the use of some form of gay slur. That's easy. It's shorthand. Many children don't even understand exactly what they are calling the other person. In their minds the word means Bad or Wrong. Education's job is to stop that. The abuse of words stems from a misunderstanding of those words. In schools we have finally reached the point that we deal with one student calling another a gay slur the same way we would deal with the n-word. Those carry the same emotional weight and can cause the same amount of damage. The difference is in everyone's mind the n-word is bad Period End of Story. It's a terrible word from an era past. Gay slurs are bad because they are saying that being homosexual is bad. Somehow that is still an idea that is it okay for people to have. Teachers need to support all children, especially the ones that might be different. We educate the ignorant. An ignorant child can be

113

helped.

A hard, unfortunate, disgusting truth about education is that children aren't the only bullies in schools. I have seen teachers bully students. I have seen teachers take their authority and abuse it. I know teachers who rejoice in the pain of a child. Those teachers will say that they are correcting behaviors, they are helping the child, they are motivating him.

They aren't.

They are being mean. They are being bullies.

It's hard to catch a teacher being a bully. Teachers, rightly so for the most part, should get the benefit of the doubt. A parent complains that the teacher is being mean to their kid and administration should look into it and get the full story, but odds are the parent is misreading the situation. When complaints pile up, though, when the administration has heard from multiple sources that certain teachers are behaving in certain ways they have to do something. I've seen students trembling in the office, refusing to go to class for fear of their teacher. That's not normal. That's not healthy. School should be a safe, happy place. Teachers who are bullies personally offend me. There aren't many, but they do exist. They team up on kids. They hammer students for small things over and over. Their discipline plans leave no room for improvement or positivity. I was once told by a pair of bullies, "We don't do positive reinforcement." I had to work with those people.

Teachers who bully try to intimidate other teachers as well. I'm not a person easily intimidated, but in my second year at a school, first year in a new grade level, I'm not going to do much boat-rocking. The louder veteran teachers drowned out the protests of those who knew they were wrong. Don't be drowned out by the evil, the loud, the disgusting. Stand up to bully teachers. Fight back. Bullies are weaker than they seem, and all it takes is some push back to reveal that truth.

Parents can prevent teacher bullying. All they have to do is talk to their students. Parents, ask how the teacher is treating your child and filter it through your Grown-Up Brain. Do these punishments seem reasonable or excessive? Does it sound like your child is telling you everything? A bully teacher tells her class she is helping them. That they are lucky to have her. She won't pick on all of them, but she will hammer certain students. This will keep other students quiet because at least she isn't picking on them. Better him than me. Be aware of what is happening in your child's class and if you have a concern speak up. Don't be intimidated by teachers. By and large we are a friendly, wonderful group. Keep us honest.

Teachers remember- **Thou Shalt Not Abuse Thy Power Over Thy Students. Thou Art A Model First And Always**.

Bullying leads to cutting, drug and alcohol abuse, and suicide. Bullying needs to be cut out of our schools like a cancer. We must treat it as a serious problem that needs to be crushed. Parent and child education needs to happen on a regular basis. Teachers should be trained on what bullying is and how to prevent it in our classrooms. Teachers should embrace all of our children with all of their differences. My classroom is a safe place because I've decided it must be a safe place and I've made it one of my top objectives every year. That is clear to my students. My students want their classroom to be safe. We don't laugh at each other, we don't tease, we don't poke fun. I have a sign in the back of my room which reads, "Students Helping Students." When we switch papers and correct work as a group the goal is to help your fellow classmate do better next time. We encourage and cheer and support. When a student can't answer a question I allow him to ask a friend. A rising tide lifts all boats.

If someone does make fun of someone else for being a girl or being weird or being different I make an example of them and we have that conversation in the open, in front of everyone. So there is no doubt.

Schools will never be completely bully-free. Bullies will always exist. That doesn't mean we shouldn't do everything in our power to take their power away. Stop bullying before it starts.

Teach understanding.

Chapter 16: Letters To Prison

Any teacher who has been teaching for more than two years has at least three stories that will make you cry. It is unavoidable.

We live in a world where sometimes terrible things happen to children. When terrible things happen to children they are a thousand times worse. While I am not saying teachers are more empathetic than other people, I will say that the bond a good teacher forms with his students makes their hurts our hurts. We see these kids every day. Students aren't, "those children at work." Students are, "my kids."

Good teachers know that even the troublemakers have a reason for being that way. Good teachers know that the hard kids are not hard because of who they are, but almost always because of who they are around. Even the stereotypical good kids have a few stories that will make the room get dusty. Perhaps I'm just more emotional than most. I read *Charlotte's Web* to my class every year, and every single year I cry at the words, "No one was with her when she died." I curse you, E.B. White. You make me cry in front of 25 nine and ten year olds.

I don't like telling sad student stories. Everyone has a bigger file of them than we care to think about. When a teacher tells too many sad student stories I begin to feel like they are trying to make me understand how empathetic of a teacher they are and how hard their job is. Maybe that's true, maybe I'm being cynical. Maybe I just would rather tell happy stories. Certainly in this book I am trying to focus on the positive. That's the name of the game in my classroom. Stay positive. That way the kids with sad stories come to school and are able to relax and be in a safe, positive place for a while. Positive places give the kids with sad stories happy stories to hold on to.

That said, one instance always comes to mind when I think about sad student stories. It doesn't come to mind because I want to try to make you, my dear reader, cry. My sad student stories serve as a reminder to me that for some of these kids school is not as important as I'd like it to be. As with most things in a child's life, this is not the child's fault. This sad student story tells me that when they go home, as much as I wish it were otherwise, some of my kids have bigger things to worry about than finishing page 45 #2-36 in the math book. I want them to finish it, but I need to understand that sometimes that just isn't going to happen. Or maybe it'll happen, but not with the effort and focus I expect. I need to understand that.

This was my first year of contracted teaching. I was at a school in Southern California. I'd spent two years in Central California, where people don't know how to drive (or so I thought until I moved to Hawaii and found out what that really means), substitute teaching and taking long term jobs before moving south, back to the town I grew up in. My school was small, much smaller than the school I would end up at the next year in the Aloha State. Demographically we were like a lot of small town Southern California schools. Very mixed between white and Mexican-Americans students. A lot of migrant families. Fifty percent of my class was some level of bilingual in Spanish and English. We were in a fairly low-income neighborhood.

We don't have grass on our field. It is dirt. We live in the desert. Sometimes it gets so windy we can't have recess because the kindergarteners would blow away and the wind whips up so much dust it would sandblast Batman right off the children's lunchboxes. When it gets like that I can't let the smaller kids open the classroom door. Their arms would come off.

I have eighteen third graders in my room. If this seems

like a small number that's because it is. California had class-size regulations through third grade and we weren't supposed to have more than twenty students. That's a beautiful thing. You have no idea how small a room of eighteen is until you have thirty-one sixth graders.

We were doing independent work. I had made a list of assignments to complete and let the students at it. I like that kind of freedom in my classroom. I think they learn to prioritize, plus it provides a simulation of choice, which everyone likes. They will get everything I want finished done, but they get to choose how and when. Everyone wins.

The class was working away and we were nearing the end of the time I'd given them when one of my little girls came up to me.

"Mr. Robertson?"

"Yes, child?"

"I'm all done."

"Ok, you know that when you're all done you read."

"I know, but instead can I write a letter to my dad? He's in prison."

No one prepares you for this question in Teacher School. I never took a class called Prison And Parents: What To Do What To Do 101. I never role-played this with a professor. So I did what any normal teacher would do. I told her of course she could write her dad in prison a letter. I'm sure he would like that very much. I tried to shake off that little glimpse into her home life, saving the information for later, and went back to roaming the room looking for wandering eyes.

A few minutes later she came back to me. "Mr. Robertson?"

"Yes?"

"Mr. Robertson...I don't know what to write. Can you help me?"

Can I help you?

119

Can I help you write a letter to your dad in prison?

...I guess so.

I mean, I know how to write a letter. You put the date and "Dear Dad," at the top and- of course that's not what she meant! I'm supposed to help this third grader communicate with her father who she hasn't seen in I don't know how long about whatever she feels is important to tell him while he's locked up and can't see her. Which he will then, I assume, read over and over again in his cell, probably crying because he can't hold his little girl and have her tell him all this in person. No. One. Taught. Me. This. I was not warned. This wasn't in the interview.

So I sat down next to her and helped her brainstorm ideas. Do you want to tell him about school? Tell him about the story we just read and how good you did on that last spelling test. Tell him how you're learning about these things in math and they are kind of hard right now but you know you'll get it. Tell him you miss him.

At recess I did a little digging. First I tried not to sob once I was alone in my room, then I did some digging. Out of my eighteen students, three had dads in jail. Three out of eighteen is a ridiculous fraction. A fifth of my kids? What about the rest of the school? What about the other kids in my class? What is going on in their homes? This was the first time those questions solidified in my head.

This is as good a time as any for a mini-soapbox. Dads? Come over here for a second-

Knock it off.

Not just with the jail stuff, I realize that's a small percentage of the whole. Still, if a parent is in prison it is probably the dad. So knock that off too. But mostly knock off the not being around. Mom should not be the only one involved in your child's education. Every Open House I get a ton a moms and a couple of dads. Every Parent Conference I get mostly moms and a few dads. Where are we, guys? We need to be better represented. As a father and a male teacher I get such a rush when a dad wants to come on a field trip, volunteer in the class, do Read Across America. I love it when another man comes into my classroom to work with the children. Dads, you need to get more involved. For your children's sake.

Thus endeth the soapboxing.

As teachers it is important for us to remember all the other things happening in our students' lives. It is important to remember that the homework we assign might seem like it is super-important, and we know it is more important than video games or football practice, but sometimes other things are more important.

Like writing a letter. And if it is important to our students, it should be important to us.

Doug Robertson

Chapter 17: Spelling Tests

Giving spelling tests is one of the best parts of my job. I love spelling tests. They would be the cream in my Friday cup of coffee if I put cream in my coffee. I love spelling tests because they are a direct opportunity for me to put Teaching is a Performance Art into wonderfully goofy action.

Spelling words can be lame and boring. Most well-written basal learners will give each spelling list a focus theme. This week we are working on words with different /f/ spellings. This week is irregular plurals. This week is homophones. This week is a seemingly random collection of 25 words because I'm not going to read the Teacher's Edition explanation of the list. Basal lists guide instruction, keep me as a teacher focused, and normally the words relate both to the story and to what the students should have learned in previous weeks.

Spelling as an assignment can be argued as irrelevant since the creation of spell check. Students love to try this at least once a year. I disagree, as will anyone who has ever been on an internet comment section or forum. People refuse to use spell check. They will seemingly willfully not notice the squiggly red line beneath their broken word. Maybe they think the computer is adding flair to the sentence. Twitter, Facebook, Firefox, Safari will all spell check your words for you, and yet it doesn't matter. As I tell my students, like it or not people will judge your intelligence by how you spell. It's easy shorthand for Does This Person Know What They Are Talking About. I realize it is shallow, but you could be making the best point in the world and if you transpose your/you're and to/too/two too many times I'm blocking you out. I'm not listening anymore. Lalalala. Spelling is how you judge people you can not hear. Too many misspellings are the written equivalent of saying, "umm," every three words.

Along with the actual list, Teacher's Editions come with sample test sentences. The reasoning being two-fold. One- your district is paying a lot of money for these books, there had better be a ton of content. Two- you would be shocked how hard it is coming up with sentences off the top of your head sometimes. Know what is even worse? Word problems. For a normal human, coming up with an interesting and relevant word problem on the spot is damn near impossible. In front of a class, while your Teacher Brain is running the hundred other subroutines it needs to run every time you are on stage (example subroutines- Who Is Talking? Where Is That Noise Coming From? Is He Back From The Bathroom Yet? Was That A Kindergartener Running Outside Again? What's That Smell?) coming up with mildly clever sentences on the spot can be a chore. Especially if you're one of those teachers who needs their classroom environment to be Very Serious Business Because School Is Serious. In that case you use the book's boring sentences because you would just come up with your own boring sentences anyway. For example- "Scrambled. I would like scrambled eggs. Scrambled." Boooorrriiinnng.

I know, I know. This is supposed to be a test. I am supposed to be evaluating my students' learning to determine the best course of action moving forward, and to that end I should take assessments seriously. But I give one of these just about every Friday. That's a lot of lame sentences. That gets old faster than plain bagels for breakfast. If I am bored with something, I know my kids are.

I have my class well trained. I make my expectations very clear from Minute One. They know how they should behave. They also know that Mr. Robertson is a little weird, and that occasionally means they are also allowed to get a little weird as long as they can pull it back together the moment I ask them to. When I get to a spelling test, I want to have fun. My class knows that doesn't mean spelling tests are play time. It simply means that spelling words can be used in creative ways.

Tangent- I was a lifeguard for the City of Palmdale for approximately 68 years while I was a teenager. I don't overstate the time because it felt like it took forever, I do it because I loved it so very much and I learned more about teaching on the deck of Courson and McAdam pool than I did in some of my college classes.

One of my responsibilities as a lifeguard was teaching swim lessons. Swim lessons were two week sessions, four days a week. On the third-to-last day of swim lessons each session we would have what was known as Safety Day. Safety Day was the day that, instead of starting classes like normal, we would line all the little swimmers up by the pool rules sign and talk about each rule and why it was important.

We did a lot of Safety Days. Once every two weeks, six times a day each time. You get bored of the regular, "Rule #1- Obey Lifeguards. Why do we obey lifeguards? Because we are trying to keep you safe," very quickly. It became a game to see who could have the best Safety Day presentation. My favorite Safety Days were called Everything Ends In Death. Here is how Everything Ends in Death goes- "Rule Number Six- Don't chew gum. Why don't we chew gum?" Now, here it would be very easy to go to, "Because you'll choke and die." That's hack. Anyone can come up with choke and die. No, a pro comes up with, "Don't chew gum because you could be swimming along and the gum might float out of your mouth and sink to the bottom of the pool and then someone else steps on it on the bottom and the gum sticks to their foot and they get stuck to the bottom and they drown and die." That, my friends, is how you play Everything Ends In Death Safety Day. This information is important in a moment. -End Tangent

My spelling tests in class must be more interesting than what the books suggests, and more fun than the lame sentences just anyone could come up with. With my spelling tests I feel I am modeling for my students the fun a person can and should have with words. Words are not precious objects to be kept on a shelf. Words are toys, words are Legos, words are there to be put in strange orders and mixed about. My spelling tests strive to be at the very least entertaining for myself and my students, and at the most free association art forms.

I have told an entire scary story using only the sentences afforded by the 25 spelling words on Halloween. That's hard. It gives you an entirely new appreciation for writers and improvisational actors, especially because I'm not going to spend time writing this story before class. It's coming as I think of it. I usually don't go to Everything Ends In Death in class, because that's a little dark for students I have to work with all year, but I will end every sentence with, "And then I cried." Trust me, nothing is funnier to a third or fourth grader than their tattooed, bearded, scowling man teacher talking about how something made him cry. It's hilarious.

"Grow- I spent a year taking care of a rose, trying to grow it as nicely as possible and it was beautiful and perfect,... and then my sister stomped on it and I cried."

I often tease kindergarteners in my class. Why? Because they are tiny insane people, that's why. So I'll spend 25 sentences detailing different ways to hunt, catch, and cook five year-olds. Note- this works only if you've had The Bullying Talk with your students and they know you're playing. Some kids don't get fooling around, but by nine or ten most do. Kids are so much smarter than adults give them credit for.

And sometimes there are the free association, crazy pants spelling tests. Remember the sentence for scrambled from above? This is an actual thing I once said to my class during a spelling test-

"Scrambled- I went to a restaurant for breakfast and I

126

ordered some eggs. The waitress asked how I would like them. 'Scrambled,' I said. 'Scrambled?' she asked. 'Scrambled,' I replied. 'Scrambled then. You sure?' she asked. 'Yes, scrambled. I would like my eggs scrambled. Not poached, fried, over easy, or raw, but scrambled.' 'So you want scrambled eggs is what you're saying?' 'Wait...let me think...Yes please, scrambled.'"

They were dying by the end. Then I had to repeat the word because one kid genuinely asked what the word he was supposed to spell was. (He got it wrong. He had all week, how could he have not known?)

Does that help them spell the word better? No. Does it teach them anything about the etymology of the word? No. It holds no obvious educational value to an outside observer.

It does make them want to come to school. It turns a test, something children are supposed to dread and fear and hate, into an enjoyable event. My class *likes taking spelling tests*. I like giving spelling tests. They associate a positive emotion with an assessment. Silly sentences don't mess up their scores. If they know the word then they get it right, it doesn't matter if we play or not. So why not play? Why not help them enjoy one more aspect of school? Why not model one more way words can be fun? They are always learning, one way or another. Best to remember that.

Doug Robertson

Chapter 18. My First Staff Meeting

No one likes meetings. No one in their right mind. They are often boring, repetitive, and drone on forever and are repetitive and drone on forever and are boring. Many times they are full of information you either don't need or already had. Or information you needed three days ago. Even talented administrators can't escape the simple fact that teachers are the worst possible audience in the world.

Think about it- All we do all day is speak in front of a group. We are the center of attention all day long. You will look at me. You will listen to me. You will respond to me. Now all those people are supposed to sit and be talked *at*?

I'm not sure what teachers (and husbands outside changing rooms) did before smart phones, but I'm glad I live when I do. This is not to say I don't pay attention during meetings, because I do. It's just that sometimes I know where this is going and I've already gotten there. The best example of this is technology meetings. There's some guy explaining a new computer program we have to learn. "Ok, first you need to open the application. Can you say application? Good. Ok, you see that little arrow, that's called the cursor. Can you say cursor? Now double-click on this icon and...why won't it open? Hold on one second."

Around me older teachers who didn't grow up with computers are frantically taking notes or checked out completely because they, "never understand this technology stuff." Meanwhile, every tech savvy teacher has already run the tutorial, texted in a snarky Facebook status update, and posted a blog about the bugs we found. Can we go home now?

I didn't always know this about staff meetings. When I started I thought grown up meetings were different than student meetings. Sure, sitting in class while my professor went on could be lame, but that's because I'm a student and he's a teacher. When I'm a teacher and the principal is talking I'll listen! Sit up straight, shoulders back, chin up, pen at the ready. The teacher can give me a bad grade. The principal could *fire me*! Better get it together, Robertson.

It was with this attitude that I went into my first staff meeting. I was a student teacher and I wanted a job when I was done with school. I showed up to the cafeteria early. I brought a notebook and a pencil. I got a good seat. I was ready.

The principal started talking and I started taking notes. I barely doodled at all. Eventually, as you do, I started looking around the room to see if everyone else was paying close attention too (and if they were noticing that I was paying such close attention because HIRE ME I WANT TO STOP SERVING SPAGHETTI TO PAY RENT). What did I see?

Those two teachers are passing notes! There are four grading papers. I don't think they've looked up once. No one is taking notes! Hey, I think that guy might be asleep! Where is that other lady? Did she skip out? Can you do that?

Opened my eyes.

You know what else was strange, and this might be something most people don't think about? Bathroom freedom. When you're a student you can't just get up and go. Maybe in some college courses, if your professor is cool. Students are good at bladder budgeting. Teachers, while they are teaching, are even better. One does not walk out on 25 nine-year olds to pee. One dances and tries to think of something else, glancing out the door for a passing aide to save you before your back teeth float away. But in a staff meeting? Teachers just get up and walk out. While someone is talking. Because hey, we're all adults here and we understand. Stress = relieved (get it?). This is also a great way to get away from a particularly obnoxious presenter for a few minutes. Not that I would ever do that. I've heard of teachers doing that. At other schools. Elsewhere. Who aren't me.

I still try and pay attention in meetings. You need to know when the principal or another teacher is trying to pull a fast one on you. What's that little piece of rule you're trying to get into the school planner? I don't think so. I watch the brand new teachers at my school sitting attentively, purposefully ignoring the blinking red light on their phones. I laugh when my principal tries to illustrate a point by using a football metaphor, not realizing that 80% of his audience doesn't know or care about the job of the middle linebacker in relation to the running back or how that relates to the new standardized test that will be introduced next year.

I've never fallen asleep in a staff meeting. I've spaced out. I've lost time. I've missed important information. But I've never fallen asleep. That should count for something.

Not to say all staff meetings are a waste of time. I've been in meetings where input was given and productive discussions were had. I imagine a smaller school can get a bunch done in a staff meeting. Less opinions to listen to. Every school, just like every college class, probably has those people who think it is their job to lengthen the meeting. Just when you think it is over, up goes the hand for another question. If you're lucky, really lucky, the question pertains to the subject at hand. Probably something that has already been covered, but at least relevant.

Good meetings, like good lessons, have plans and goals. They keep time in mind and are run efficiently by someone who acts like they are in charge. There's some humor to keep me, the audience, entertained and interested. There's good information. If there is a discussion element we have a reason to speak up, we're encouraged to say interesting things and the presenter knows how to deal with off topic digressions. And lastly, there's an end in sight. I don't want to be glancing at the clock every two minutes, and the presenter doesn't want to see me doing that.

My first staff meeting was enlightening because I realized just how free some schools let their grown-ups be. Some principals don't fly that way and are very tight on everyone. That's up to the administrator. Like a good student, I'll try to get away with whatever I'm allowed while still being a part of the meeting. My job as a teacher is to care, but your job as a presenter is to make me care.

Chapter 19: What I Want Out of an Administrator

I'm a relatively young teacher. I will be looking for jobs long after this book comes out. I've written a chapter about administrators. I may not be as bright as I think I am.

I do not want to be an administrator. The more I learn about the job, the worse it sounds. Administrators have an incredibly tough job, and the juggling act they have to perform is analogous to balancing on a unicycle while keeping a chainsaw, a machete, a baby, a machete-wielding baby, and a flaming poodle in the air. Administrators are thinking about the teachers below them, the superintendents above them, the standards being imposed on them, the test scores judging them, the parents coming to them, and always the students around them. That's a lot on one person's plate. Two or three people if your school is lucky enough to have a VP or two.

I do not envy principals' their job. From what I can gather it is not a happy place. I get to teach all day. I see students at their best. The only time a principal sees a student is when the child is in trouble. That's a huge bummer. One of the reasons I teach is I like working with children more than I like working with adults. A principal deals almost exclusively with adults. Much like the children they see, the adults they see are either upset, in trouble, or both. Angry parents and teachers stream in and out of a principal's office daily. I would not want to spend my day disciplining teachers and talking parents down. At my first job my co-teacher and I were constantly in our principal's office complaining about things. It got to the point where I felt like we were Frank Burns and Margaret Houlihan (minus the sexual tension) bothering Col. Potter. (My principal at the time was much too smart to be Col. Blake.) I wouldn't want to be on that side of the desk. I want to go back to my classroom and my kids.

Principals do paperwork all the time. Ick. Paperwork is the bane of my existence as it is; I can't imagine what it must be like for administration. Signing things, reading notes, approving emails, checking flyers. Report cards for students are bad enough; principals have to observe and grade teachers. I'll get into evaluations later, but sitting an unsatisfactory adult down for a serious conversation has to be worse than having the same talk with a child. I know for a fact that some adults would react the same as a petulant child, with the kicking and groaning and foot stomping.

All that being said, I do have some advice for principals from a teacher's perspective. The most important of which is I want my principal to be a leader. Correction- I want my principal to be a Leader. You are the head of the school and that means you should have the strongest vision of what the school should be. If I'm right and my classroom reflects me as a teacher, then as a principal the school reflects you. That's hard, because you're dealing with a big group of adults. Adults are harder to change than children. We are harder to motivate. We feel we can complain more and louder. Many fear change. Nevertheless, the school reflects you and your style.

Being a Leader means being able to clearly express your vision for the school *and* get us to buy into it. I want to hear what you want the school to be. I want to hear how you're going to do it. More than that, then I want you to DO it. I don't know if I would be a good administrator. I think I'd chase a lot of teachers off in my first year or two. I believe in discussion, but I also believe that at some point discussion needs to stop and action needs to start. I've seen too many staff meetings stalled by questions and debate. The principal needs to be willing to say, "This is where we are going. This is how we are getting there. Either get on or get off."

I don't want to be friends with my principal. If I am then

that's great, bonus, but it's not what I'm interested in. I want to respect my administrator. I want to believe what she says she is going to do is what she actually does. Down to the ground and without a doubt. Does that mean a principal shouldn't be open to other opinions? Of course not. Bring me your ideas in a respectful, helpful way. But if I'm in charge and you question me in front of the entire staff we are going to have words. I would expect my staff to bring questions and concerns to me in private, where we can have a reasonable discussion. Having a strong vision and being an inflexible jerk are different things.

I want my principal to back me up in front of parents. I have never had an administrator question my methods during a parent meeting and I hope I never do. If he thinks I'm wrong I hope he tells me before or after the meeting. I hope he tells me at all. I don't work well with passive-aggressive people. I'm not good with subtle. I want a principal who tells me what she wants straight up. This does not mean the administrator is confrontational, but it does mean she is honest. She acts like an adult when there are issues.

Being an administrator, much like being a teacher, comes with built-in respect. I respect you because of your position. You've earned implicit respect by rising to that place in the food chain. However, if Star Trek has taught me anything it's that just because someone is a higher rank doesn't mean they are more capable. Starfleet is riddled with incompetent admirals. You'd think the Federation would have ways to prevent that. Maybe an evaluation system of some kind. It's always the guy with more pips on his collar getting the Enterprise into trouble, though.

You come with respect, but you need to maintain it, just like I come to my students expecting to be respected, but my in-class performance had better reflect that I want to keep it. I expect my administrator to be strong and stick to his stated goals. I also expect her to deal with challenges within the school setting quickly and smoothly.

I've worked for principals who are very interested in the entire staff being invested in what he wants to do. Too invested. Every staff meeting would turn into a long debate and discussion. Any dissenting opinion needed to be heard and gone over with fine grade sandpaper until all rough edges are smoothed away. To an extent I agree with that. If I have a problem I want to have my say. We are a team here. When the discussion slows forward movement to a crawl it becomes a problem. That is the point when I expect a strong leader to stop discussion and move forward with what he wants.

That might be surprising. I would rather an administrator do what he wants than listen to me talk about what I want endlessly? Yes. His job is to move forward with what he sees as best for the entire school. He shouldn't expect 100% buy-in. I don't know if you can get a big group of adults to agree on one thing, big or small. Try to plan lunch in a group bigger than five. Andy is always going to complain about Mexican food. Either everyone goes to Subway like Andy *always* wants or the group goes to Mexican and Andy can choose to come with or drive himself. I won't take it personally if the administrator moves without everyone's ok.

I think that comes from my background as an athlete. I'm used to a coach telling me, "This is what you are going to do. This is how you're going to do it. Go." I don't want that outside influence directly impacting what happens inside my classroom. I should be free to accomplish my principal's goals my own way. Outside of my classroom, in planning meetings yes, tell me what to do. I see that as your job. I'll get it done. If my principal asks my opinion on something I'm going to give it, honest and to the point. I'm not going to be worried about what the principal thinks of my opinion, she asked for it so I assume she wants it. If my principal asks me to do something I don't want to do I'm going to say no. Don't ask me. Tell me. If my administrator tells me what he wants me to do I'll do it. If I have a serious problem with it I'll ask about it in private. This might make me sound like a good little worker drone, and that's not the case. I wouldn't describe myself like that at all. I would say that I trust my administrator to do what's best by the school as a whole. There might be a plan going on that I'm not completely aware of. I'd hope he told us the plan. I've had principals go over the school budget line by line during a staff meeting. I don't need that. I don't need to know what the money situation for the school is. I trust that no one is embezzling funds. It isn't like we have much money to take anyway. Going over the budget feels like wasting time better spent doing something which will move the school forward. Going over the school plan, that's more important. Make me internalize it. Make me love it as much as you do.

The pressure is on principals for their schools to perform to expectations, no matter how silly those expectations might be. When the state or federal sword comes down they are at the top of the hit list. I know it's not an easy job. As a teacher I want to help make it as easy as possible. I will volunteer for every after school project I can. I'll come in early and stay late to help my school succeed. I'll lead my committee and show up to coach teams, referee Robotics, clean up the campus, and attend meetings. I do that because that's how I would expect my staff to act were I the principal. In return I want help, I want respect, and I want straight-up honesty. We aren't peers and I don't want to be. I want Leadership.

You be good at being in charge. You Lead. I'll follow and support. Together, with both of us doing our best, our school will rise to any challenge and conquer any peak.

Doug Robertson

Chapter 20: Learn From Fear/Inspire With Love

My way is not the only way. My way might not be the best way. But my way works for me. I will argue for my way of teaching with all my breath. Not to convert you, but to make you understand why I am the way I am, and in the hopes you see something of value in it to take as your own.

Students are going to learn no matter how you teach. Anyone who tells you differently should find another job. From the highest of the high kids to the lowest of the low, all of them are going to learn something during their time in your class. How and how much, that's up to you, the teacher.

There are thousands of theories on how to teach math and reading and writing. Books upon books, trainings after trainings, conferences atop expensive conferences. Each full of strategies and tools which range from amazingly, where-was-this-when-I-was-in-school helpful, to mind-bendingly boring and useless. The first time a speaker at my school demonstrated Singapore Math my jaw hit the table. If I'd known that when I was in elementary and middle school I probably wouldn't have been in remedial math in high school. Seriously, if you teach and you don't know Singapore math go look it up. It's great.

I think it's obvious by now that this book has no intention of teaching you, my wonderful reader, tricks for getting your students to hit specific benchmarks. I'm not trying to impart lesson plans on you. My purpose from page one has been to help you, my smart, good-looking reader, see the profession of teaching in a different light. To see what we do in a more positive way and to help you build relationships with your students.

In my school we talk about The Three Rs. No, not those three Rs. These actually all start with the letter R- Rigor.

Relevance. Relationships. I don't know what it says about us as a system that of the original three Rs only one actually starts with an R.

Rigor, Relevance, and Relationships are, according to the State of Hawaii, the three legs of the stool that is a good education. If a teacher is able to accomplish these three Rs on a regular basis that teacher will be successful in his or her goals. I don't dispute that. In fact, I agree with it. It is a general enough statement when you parse it down that it is exceedingly easy to agree with. There's nothing in the Three Rs to argue about. It sounds as though it were developed by a committee for the purpose of being put on signs and flyers. That's fine, that's what Department of Education committees are for.

Every teacher who hears the Three Rs puts them in an internal order from most to least important. That doesn't mean all three aren't important, it just means leveling things is something humans do. If I have to be thinking about these things in my classroom I have to choose which to be thinking about the most, the second most, and then the third most. Even the Three Laws of Robotics acknowledge that the First law must take precedence over the Second, both of which take precedence over the Third. (If you don't know what I'm talking about then after you finish this go read *I, Robot* by Isaac Asimov. You'll learn about teaching there too.)

When I hear Rigor, Relevance, and Relationships I automatically re-ordered them to Relationships, Relevance, Rigor. Without a doubt, having good Relationships with my students is the most important part of my teaching. I don't want to be their friend, but I do want to be friendly with them. Having a positive relationship means students look up to me, they count on me, and they respect me.

Some of you out there, and many teachers I know personally, disagree. They'll put one of the other two in front and Relationships will almost always come last. It does feel like the least important of the three.

It's the most important.

Students will learn out of fear. If you intimidate your class, if you're one of those teachers who disciplines hard and fast, your class will learn. Teachers who scare their students have quiet, working classrooms. Their kids turn in work on time, except when they don't. Their students raise their hands quietly, and rarely forget to do so. Their students perform well on standardized tests. From the outside they have an efficient, well run classroom.

But they don't have a relationship with their students. Their kids don't care about the learning. The class is quiet because they've seen what happens when you talk out of turn. You get nailed to the wall. The class turns in work on time, except when they don't, because they know hard punishment is waiting. They don't want to stay in from recess, write reflections, or go to the office. The class doesn't *ever* talk back. Out loud. They know they should respect their teacher unconditionally, and if they do not, if they even seem like they are thinking about not, their behavior will be punished. Students who work out of fear can be seen sitting outside of class, where they can't learn, during a lesson, and they can be seen sitting inside of class during recess, where they can't expend any of the energy that is keeping them from focusing. Students who learn out of fear almost always have the best lines when they walk through school. Straight, quiet lines. Lines you could use to check how level a painting is. Lines that pass by your classroom like ninjas in the night. As long as their teacher is right by them. Those lines are very different when the source of fear isn't close by.

Students who work out of fear turn in the work that is expected of them on time or they get punished. So most of the time they turn in their work. The work of frightened students is normally good, neat, on point, and on time. The work of frightened students is exactly what was asked of them. If the work isn't done you can tell. Frightened students are the ones with tears in their eyes before the opening bell even rings because they know what is waiting for them in class. They are the ones frantically scribbling down answers in the pre-bell morning lines. They will turn in something. It might not be their best work, but at least it is something. It might be enough to get away with it. To not get shouted at.

Frightened students aren't thrilled about school. School is work, it's the place they go. But they are here. They are ready to be taught at. They love the weekends. They would sprint for the door at the last bell if they weren't sure that too would lead to harsh punishment.

Frightened students will learn. And it is pretty easy to frighten students. It doesn't take much work to intimidate sixth graders, let alone first or second graders. If you put your mind to it you can cow a room full of students pretty effectively within the first week of school. Your classroom will do well on the tests, they will be complimented in assemblies for being quiet by other teachers. You'll probably have a permanent scowl fixed on your face all day and you might not enjoy your job too much, but you'll have iron-fisted control of your class. Teaching and learning will be rigorous, which isn't in the spirit of the that particular R, but it's close enough, right? Control means it is easier to get Rigor and Relevance through their heads.

I, on the other hand, believe in building Relationships first. Everything in my classroom, everything I do, is geared towards making my class a safe, welcoming, warm place for children. That doesn't mean I've got posters of kittens and clouds on my walls and it doesn't mean students in my class don't occasionally get yelled at. It does mean that if I see a student crying because of something I did I'm probably not going to be happy about it.

I'm going to go ahead and use the L-word here. Love. I want my kids to love coming to school. I don't need them to love me, but I want them to love the idea of our classroom. I want them to feel that I care for them. I care about them as people, as individuals who will someday grow into productive members of society, and they should know that. I want them to know that I don't see them as numbers on a test print-out. I'm in front of them day after day because I'm interested in their development as a whole person, not only as a student.

My lines aren't always straight and quiet. I've taught them to walk in straight, quiet lines and they can. Normally they do. But they aren't petrified of what might happen if they don't. The worst that could happen is we go back to class and try again or tomorrow at recess we practice walking straight and quiet around the basketball court for five minutes until they've proven to me they know what I expect and can do it. The punishment matches and corrects the improper behavior. If I need them to walk somewhere and I have to hang back, I can trust they will get there quietly because I've taught them to respect themselves and to respect other classes. They know their behavior reflects on them and me both.

My classroom is rarely silent. My students know to raise their hands but sometimes they forget. If they forget I ignore what was called out. Unless I forget too because we're having a good discussion. I have a lot of group work happening in my room. Three or four or five brains are better than one. Learning to work in groups is valuable because they'll need those skills later in life. Interpersonal communication is an important asset. It isn't cheating if everyone comes to the answer together. That doesn't mean my class is wildly out of control. Sometimes it might seem that way from the outside, but for the most part nothing happens in my room that I don't want to happen. I want it to be noisy and messy. That is what learning looks like to me. I get twitchy in silent rooms. I've invested the time in teaching my class that I expect them to be able to go from talkative group work to silently looking at me in, "5, 4, 3, 2, 1." We practice until we get it right and we all know that if they can't handle it I'll go the other way with noise and no one will be happy. Our relationship includes an understanding that I would rather them be happy and they would rather me be happy.

In the cafeteria and in assemblies they are quiet and respectful. I've told them that is what I expect. I've also told them I know they can do it. My class is always expected to be the best class in the school. My class can always be the quietest, the most polite, and have the best questions or answers. Because my class is full of the best kids. It's true. Every year. I tell them so, that way they know why my expectations are so lofty.

I don't want to disappoint my students. They don't want to disappoint me. My class works hard because of the relationship we've built. It says that we work for each other. They don't do good work because I'll yell at them if they fail to. They do good work because I expect them to do good work. I expect them to do work that they would be proud of, work that I can be proud to show to someone else. I hang student work on my walls and they want their work to go up. It makes the child proud. That means my students, students who learn out of love, will go above and beyond what they are asked. Not because I'll jump down their throats if they don't, but because they want to be proud of their work. Students who learn out of love will be inspired to try harder because they know their teacher doesn't punish mistakes. I ask for mistakes. I can teach mistakes. A mistake means effort was made. When a student isn't afraid in class they are more willing to take risks. They are more willing to try.

A student in a classroom that holds Relationships to the highest will put Rigor into their work because they want to. They are motivated to work harder. Relevance is up to the teacher. I can make my lessons as rigorous as I want, but if my kids don't care it doesn't matter.

Wouldn't you rather have a room where the students know you care about them? Where you smile more than you frown and laugh more than you scold? Children will learn from fear, but they will try and be inspired through love.

Doug Robertson

Chapter 21: Getting a Tie and Losing My Music

I have never been cool. I accept that. Coolness is not a state I aspire to. I am impossibly uncool. I can pretend at cool, my students may think I'm cool, but I am not cool. It's an act.

I ride a motorcycle to school. Cool teacher. I have tattoos, some of which I'm unable to hide from the children. Cool teacher. I have long hair and an interestingly groomed goatee. Cool teacher. I play music like The Beatles for the children. Cool teacher.

I wear a tie and slacks to work every day. I give homework. I sit at a desk stacked high with paper. I have a favorite whiteboard marker. I am the children's first representation of The Man. UNCOOL.

I never wanted to wear a tie to work every day. Ever since high school I've been a heavy metal guy. A headbanger, if you will. Some of my best friends play in a metal band. Nearly every CD in my car involves screeching guitars and screaming, angry young men. I can have a full-length detailed conversation with you about the lyrics of Iron Maiden songs and why they are more brilliant than you give them credit for. If you're one of those people who claims to like "all music" I have half a dozen CDs I know you'll hate within thirty seconds.

I love heavy metal.

And I teach tiny humans.

This, it feels to me, is a sort of paradox. When one drives to school cranking Marilyn Manson one puts one's self in a certain kind of mindset. Not in a bad way, and not in a way that negatively impacts my teaching. In a way that adds intensity and energy to my classroom persona. Remember, my whole philosophy on teaching boils down to "Bombastic rockstar frontman of a neverending education funk machine."

Having good music in my head and in my belly helps to propel that idea forward. Slayer at 7am does intensifying things to a person.

When I got my first contract job in California I had a male principal. He dressed sharp. I stole almost everything I know about dressing nice from how he dressed the year I worked for him. It sounds funny now, but it was from watching him that I realized how a tie goes with a shirt goes with slacks. I own a lot of black shirts, and Ward helped me see which ties wouldn't make me look like a member of The Cure's fan club. He was always well put together. He was also an excellent principal.

There were three male teachers at that school when I was there. That's a huge number for a small elementary school. Ward, the aforementioned principal, pulled us aside one day before the year started and said, "Guys, I can't tell you how to dress. I'm not allowed. I can tell you that I really like it, and I think it looks very professional, when male teachers wear ties to work." Check, gotcha boss. That afternoon I went out and bought ties. That night, with the help of my step-dad and the internet, I finally learned how to tie them.

They make ties for guys like me. I bought a tie with a big picture of Hendrix on it. I got a tie with my university's logo (Go Pacific Tigers!) emblazoned in the center. I bought Dr. Seuss ties and Star Trek ties and Star Wars ties and motorcycle ties and Aerosmith ties. If it was a non-traditional tie I wanted it. Then I'm wearing a tie, but gosh darn it, I'm not part of the machine.

My own lame little neckwear rebellion.

Eventually, though, I wanted to look nicer. More professional. There's a thing that happens when you start to dress nice. You start to feel nicer. You feel more professional. My students looked at me in a different way when I dressed sharp. Well fit slacks, clean button up shirt, nice tie, uncomfortable shiny shoes. I started to feel like I needed to make this look mine.

So I also bought nice ties. I went to the store and browsed the tie racks. So many colors. Some of them are shiny, some flat. Too many with patterns, I don't want a tie with patterns, that's not me. As I looked at the ties I started running my dress shirts through my head. Would this go with that? Should I spend this much on a tie that will only really work with one shirt? I could always buy another shirt. Teachers almost get paid enough to have fantasies about extravagant purchases like another dress shirt.

Then I found one. A Great Tie. A deep red with a slight sheen. Would be great with the black and dark-colored shirts I have, and I could probably make it work with one or two others. It needs a tie tack. Tie tacks look nice. I located a good one, one of the chain type that clip to the button behind it. Now my tie won't fly up in the wind. Great. I excitedly took my finds to the cash register waiting to ring me up. I'm going to look brilliant. Won't the boss be impressed with my tie?

It wasn't until I got in the car that I realized what I'd done. I'd gotten *excited about buying a tie*. Unironically, unself-consciously, totally honestly excited about buying a tie. My heart sank. I never was cool, but this is different. This isn't even metal. In my head I pictured what happened in my house. I knew it had to be true. As I was buying the tie, as I was excitedly picking it out and whipping out my wallet, someone was breaking into my room. A shadowy figure. Its hand reaches out, grazing my wall of CDs, searching. Searching. I swipe my debit card and the hand finds what it's looking for. A Pantera CD. The live album, one of the best live recordings ever. So brutal. The hand removes the CD and I grab the bag with my newly purchased tie. And as I turn to walk away from the counter the hand puts new music in place of my Pantera CD. It would be there, waiting for me when I got home. Mocking me. A Best of Kenny G album. Nooooooooooooooooooooooo!

I know it's silly. But being excited about buying a tie made me feel old and lame. I've mostly come to grips with it now. In fact, teaching in Hawaii no one wears a tie. The only people on the island who wear ties are guys who work in fancy restaurants or jewelry shops. Lawyers wear aloha shirts. In my time there I fell out of tie-wearing. When I got the job I asked my Grade Level Chair over the phone what the dress code for the school was. "I normally wear ties, dress shirts, and slacks to school. Is that ok?" She laughed at me. "You could, but you'll be better dressed than the principal." So I wore polos or short sleeve collared shirts and cargo pants. I was still one of the nicer dressed teachers. I don't wear shorts.

We had Dress Nice Day at during Spirit Week, and I decided to really go for it. I always dress up for the Spirit Week Days, Pajama Day, Sports Day, Wacky Hair Day, it's fun. The kids like it when their teachers dress up. I figure that I don't want the students to act Too Cool to do something, so I shouldn't either. If dressing up for Pajama Day is going to ruin my classroom discipline or my students' respect for me, then those things never existed in the first place. The night before Dress Nice Day I pulled out my nice slacks, my button up shirts, found a tie or two, and tried everything on. Nothing fit. I wasn't heavy in California, but I was lifting a lot of weights and not doing much cardio. Since I moved to Hawaii I started doing triathlons and not lifting weights. My waist size has changed. Everything hung like a tent. The wife and I went shopping to get me some stylish and formal new threads. I also bought a punk rock CD for balance, a habit I picked up years ago to fight the encroaching Old And Lame.

I found, coming to school dressed formally again, that I liked it. At some point I'd grown accustomed to formalwear and looking professional. I like the way students react to a man in slacks and a tie. Here's the thing- a lot of children have little to no positive experience with men dressed nicely. You know where they see them? Courtrooms. On TV as the bad guy. As cops. So when their favorite teacher comes to school dressed up they are impressed. I'm teaching them, even when I'm not saying a word. I'm modeling for the boys ways they can look nice, ways they look professional. I'm modeling for the girls that men who dress up are good things. Both groups note that someone they look up to takes pride in his appearance and dresses like it. They don't know that I'm not cool. They are nine and ten. They still think I'm awesome. They have no idea I speak Klingon. All they know is I can dress like this and ride my motorcycle to school. I can dress like this and still be a bombastic rockstar frontman of a neverending education funk machine.

Doug Robertson

Chapter 22: Strange Things I Do In My Classroom (OR Things I Think I Might Have Stolen)

Every teacher has a grab bag of sponge lessons and random acts of education they do in their room. I would give credit for the ones I'm going to talk about if I could, but I don't remember where or who most of the ideas come from. As I tell my student teachers, steal everything. Why reinvent the wheel? Someone else has already taught this, you simply have to find it.

Switches to Old Man Mode You youngsters have it so easy now. When I started teaching Google didn't aggregate everything that you wanted into an easy-to-sort mass. You had to go into other teachers' rooms and rip them off directly. Taking notes right under their noses. And we didn't have cell phones to take pictures of projects. We had to make our own papyrus and do charcoal sketches. Now people post lessons online and you can just find them. For free! *Old Man Mode deactivated*

Teaching is all about theft. I might have a good idea, you might have a good idea, we should be willing to share our good ideas. My idea might work for your students, and vice versa. These are some of the odd things I do in my room to keep my students occupied, to create a learning environment conducive to my style, and to keep myself sane.

Storytime- Creativity is key in my classroom, and I love how creative children can be. I want to encourage and nurture that. The hardest part of coming up with a story, often, is starting it. So I play a game called Storytime with them that takes that out of the equation.

I have an inflatable ball in my room. I use it for all kinds of things, but I find it gets most often used for Storytime. Inflatable balls are a good classroom tool because you can toss them around, but they are impossible to throw hard with any accuracy and they don't hurt when they bounce off your face. No one has ever gone to the nurse with an inflatable ball-related injury.

I start the Storytime story. Sometimes I give the students a genre, sometime I leave it free. That wholly depends on if we are working on a specific genre in class or if the mood takes me. The story in my class is always about Stu. Stu is an in-class character I stole from a professor in college...I think. I might have stolen him from a middle school teacher I had. Stu's full name is Stu Dent. The moment they see Stu's full name written out the for first time is always a bright spot of that day. "Ohhhhhhhh!" I use Stu whenever I want to make a point or tell a hypothetical story. When we go over the class rules at the beginning of the year Stu is always my culprit. Stu gets in trouble a lot. Stu takes all the tests and I use his paper to correct when we go over the answers. Yes, I correct tests with my class as a whole. We switch papers first. How else will they know what they got wrong and why? Stu always remembers to put his name on his work. Stu, I tell them, is my only friend. When I draw Stu I draw a stick figure. They are not allowed to draw stick figures because that is not how people look. I can because I'm drawing Stu, and that is how Stu looks. Stop judging Stu. He's always been painfully thin. He's very sensitive about it.

Stu is the main character of our Storytime stories. I'll begin, "Stu went to the beach." The children wave their hands in the air like they care quite a bit. I call a name and gently toss the ball to her. Always call the name, that way there is no fighting over who the intended target was. The child with the ball gets to say the next sentence of the story. If she doesn't catch the ball the person who does hands it nicely to her.

There are no interceptions, or your round is over. After she says the next sentence of the story she calls a name and passes the ball.

The worst things happen to Stu. He's been eaten more times than I can count. He's been dropped out of airplanes and hit by comets and stung by a cloud of wasps. I'll often have to make a rule that Thou Shalt Not Kill Stu. "Awwwwwww, Mr. Robertson." Stuicide is fun. The game then becomes Seriously Injure Stu Who Miraculously Recovers.

Storytime does have rules. No non-sequiturs. Each part of the story must logically follow the previous part. It is so much fun to watch a kid try to set up an action only to have the next kid go in a totally different direction. The story does not end until I say The End Is Nigh. That's the signal that the next pass is the final pass.

Storytime can be as long or as short as you like. It can be strictly regimented inside a genre or free to flow between them. Stu stories can be funny or sad or a little of both. You get to dictate all of that. Someday I'll record a year's worth of Stu Stories for a book. The poor guy deserves that much.

Tableau- I don't know if I stole Tableau or if I came up with it on my own. I think I took Charades and mucked around with it until it worked like I wanted for the lesson I was teaching. I was looking for a way to teach vocabulary in a more interactive, involving manner. I had grown tired of word, definition, part of speech, synonym, antonym, sentence-type lessons. My general outlook on that is if I'm tired of something then the students are most definitely tired of it. Time for a change!

My goal was to get my students out of their desks and moving around. They don't do enough of that. Movement-based learning is underutilized in school, and I needed to fix that for myself. These kids are hams; I know they like to get up out of their seats, let's see if we can't do something with that.

The first time I had my class do Tableau I was making it up as I went. I had a basic idea of what the lesson would be, but I figured things would have to change as I went so I might as well leave it loose. The idea of working without a net is the kind of teaching experiment I enjoy. What's the worst that can happen? I find a lesson that needs to be fixed. Every time after has been basically the same because that first time went well.

First, we clear the desks. This is a procedure we practice a lot in my class. Take the groups, break them up, move them all to the perimeter of the room leaving as much center space as possible. I'm in a portable and don't have a ton of room to begin with, so we end up working with what space we can make. Clearing desks is a game in and of itself. How quickly and silently can you do it? Can you do it in under x time limit? Don't knock anything over. Don't tip anything out. Set expectations high but achievable for your class and they will meet them.

Once the desks are cleared they gather at my feet and I explain the lesson. They will work in their groups and choose four of their seven vocabulary words. They will have to choose a pose which they think best demonstrates that word because the rest of the class is going to have to guess what their tableau is representing. They may not talk. They may move slowly into each position but when I say, "Freeze," everyone has to hit their proper spot. I then call out, "Guess," and the students watching get to guess which word is being shown. Once a correct guess is made I say, "Next," and the group, without speaking, has to move seamlessly into their next word and the whole thing starts over.

What I like best about this assignment is it doesn't feel like it should work when you first think about it. Some vocabulary words do not lend themselves to physical representations. It makes the students think deeply about the words. They have to work together. I give them plenty of time to discuss and practice before we come together as a group. I monitor discussions and give tips where I think they are needed. We talk about levels, high, middle, low, before breaking into groups so they know I expect them to use all three and I know they know what all three are. It's fun and it gets words into their heads in a new and different way, hopefully in a way that will lodge them there better than mere rote learning would. It also works for any subject. Ask a group of fourth graders to show you fraction or economics without speaking or moving. They can do it if you give them the time and faith.

Watching You- Watching You isn't a game and it isn't a lesson. It's not active at all. The point of Watching You is to constantly remind my students and myself that learning is serious business, but it doesn't have to be taken seriously. It is easy to explain. I know I stole it, but I don't know who from.

Before the school year starts I take a picture of myself looking stern- arms crossed, scowling at the camera. I print five full-page copies of the picture, which I put into clear protective covers. Then I staple the pictures to the walls of my classroom, one on each wall and one on the ceiling.

I say nothing about the pictures. I do not acknowledge them in any way until a student does. This doesn't take long. The one in the front of the classroom doesn't get noticed first because it's normally hidden behind the pull-down screen. It'll be one to the side first seen. I hear it discovered. "What the..hey! There's a picture of Mr. Robertson over here!" Eyes immediately go to the picture, then to the opposite wall, where they find the other. "Hey! He's over here too!"

Quickly they look to the back of the room and see me staring down at them. "He's got pictures all over the place!" They think discoveries are over now. Where else would a picture be? When I roll up the screen to reveal number four it gets a delighted scream from the class. "Why do you have pictures of yourself all over the room?"

"Because I'm always watching you."

It isn't until later that someone finds the one on the ceiling. That's the best one. The child is becoming bored with class. He lets his head loll back. What in the what? "He's on the ceiling!"

It's great. It works all year as parents and other classes come to my room for various reasons. Keeps me amused. It's funny to listen to the kids share it with siblings outside of class. "He's got pictures of himself all over! I know, it's weird, right?"

Music- I abhor a silent classroom. I loathe it. A totally silent classroom means someone is plotting something. It freaks me out. Standardized testing days are the worst. Stressed children staring at computer screens for hours. Sitting at my desk monitoring them, trying not to look at the questions because I don't want to know. Even normal work time can't be too quiet for me. I need something.

So I play music. I cannot play the music from my car. Even the most tolerant principal will not be pleased with my blasting Slayer at the children. I play quieter, calmer music. Music I don't know if they'll hear anywhere else. When my students are being good and working quietly I play the Beatles. Because the Beatles are the best and the children should learn that as early as possible. Some sing along, which is cool because they know the songs, but uncool in that they should be focused on working. I do not encourage singing along under normal circumstances. I also do not stop it if the singer is still getting good work done.

If I think a vocal track might be distracting I go to jazz or classical. My classes, whether they know it or not, have heard jazz classics like Miles Davis's Kind of Blue and selections of Sonny Rollins. I have Pandora radio stations dedicated to Mozart and Beethoven for when I'm feeling extremely old school.

Students should be exposed to varieties of music early. It increases the likelihood their tastes will be expansive. Sometimes they ask me if they can bring in music. I say no. I'm not interested in their music. I play music I want to hear. I play music I want them to hear. My class is a benevolent dictatorship. I am King Disc Jockey.

Pen Pals- I'm not the first person to come up with Pen Pals. A ton of teachers do Pen Pals. Do they do them in a different language though?

A friend of mine from college went to Japan to teach and thanks to the magic of Facebook we were able to stay in touch. He was looking for an American class for his kids to practice their English with; I'm always on the lookout for interesting things for my kids to do and Hawaii is very nearly America, so we got together. It was very cool.

Letters from Japan would come in, brightly colored and happy. The Japanese students would write their letters in Japanese, and their teacher would go through and help them translate the letters into English. Most of my students have never seen Japanese written down before. Blew their young brains. It's such a pretty written language. Of course they all want to reply in Japanese. Two problems- (1) None of my students know Japanese. (2)The guy who teaches my students doesn't know Japanese. Translation programs are good, but not that good.

So we improvised. My friend helped with the translations by writing the English directly above the characters. I told my students to look at the words they wanted to write in their rough drafts and see if there are any matches between their words and the Japanese characters. From there they could make an educated guess at the proper character. I warned my friend that it was entirely possible he was about to get 25 letters that made sense in English, but would occasionally say, "sink rabbit classroom video game run soccer name," in Japanese.

Having pen pals in Japan also meant that we got to look into the culture a little, do some independent investigations of the island nation, and learn about things that aren't exactly in the standards but who cares because my kids were interested and this interest will translate to other subjects. They want to learn. That should be a standard. Writing a friendly letter is a standard, so there's that box checked.

We sent nearly half a dozen letters back and forth. Not bad with everything else that needs to happen in classrooms. The kids kept all their letters. I know a few asked mom and dad if they could go to Japan on their next vacation to meet their new friend. Sometimes being a teacher means planting ideas in a child's head and then sending them home for the parents to deal with.

Imaginary Class Pet- I don't have a class pet. It's a pain and I don't want to be responsible for a bunny or a guinea pig or other small furry mammal. Or a fish, mostly because fish are boring pets. Over breaks and weekends I'm the one who would have to care for Fluffy and I'm not interested. Enter Imaginary Class Pet. This is an idea I have that I've yet to put into practice. It sounds like fun though.

I'd have my students design the animal. Maybe give each group a body part and then combine them into some horrible mutant hybrid we can call our own. We would have to design a care and feeding plan for the animal. I'd give the job to someone in class, maybe a few someones, and it would be their responsibility to take care of the animal. I'd spring for a cage or tank, depending on what we decided the animal needed for living conditions. That would be fun, an empty tank in the room all year with a name tag on it. My students are goofy, I know they would introduce class visitors to the empty cage. They would play and pretend they could see him and look how cute he is and watch out he's getting grumpy. We would do writing assignments and art assignments about our Imaginary Class Pet. We would integrate science so we could talk about what our pet might eat and why. Where he might live and why. What kind of conditions are needed inside his tank and why. I'd make them justify every decision, explain every choice. Maybe by fourth quarter each group could have a small cage along the back wall in which they keep their own Imaginary Class Pet.

I like this idea. I think I'm going to try it next year. At least a hybrid mutant won't stink as bad as a bunny.

Doug Robertson

Chapter 23: Special Guests

Once a guy with a throat tattoo did a lesson for my third graders.

I should go back a few steps.

It is of the utmost importance to me that I am not the only person to speak to my class over the course of the year. I know I am not the Sole Voice of Knowledge, and so should they. Having guest speakers in the classroom allows me, their teacher, to sit back and watch from the outside how they deal with someone talking with them. It provides me with another valuable perspective on my students. Who is spacing out? More importantly, who is spacing out that I didn't expect to space out? Who is in the back of the room digging in their desk? Why haven't I noticed that before? Do they do it with me too, or only with new people? Probably with me too. I need to get better at watching that child from now on. Who looks attentive? Who is asking questions? These are all observations that are harder to make when I'm the one teaching. Having a guest allows me opportunities to see more, learn more, and be better at my job.

Guest speakers have a more substantial purpose, though, than allowing me to sit back and watch my class watch someone else. They allow my class the chance to meet someone new, to be exposed to different viewpoints, attitudes, and styles. Children should learn to be flexible in their learning, and a great way to teach them to do that is to bring in other people to teach them. If you're lucky your school has that built into the system. You have a computer teacher, a librarian and maybe, just maybe, if you're crazy lucky, a music teacher or art teacher. Oh, how wonderful an art teacher would be.

I send my children to those people to learn from them for a while, and they come back to me with renewed interest and perhaps appreciation of the way things are done in our class. Or with suggestions on how I could do it better. That happens too. I will occasionally have the brave child who tells me she likes how some other teacher does their thing more than how I do it. I take that into consideration. If she's bringing it up she's not trying to make me feel bad, she's trying to communicate something to me. Not every child responds to my default teaching setting, and it is up to me to find ways to get them to respond. That includes listening to them talk about other teachers.

What I really like is to bring in outside people to speak to the children. Those guest speakers are the best. Finding creative, interesting people to speak to the class is a never-ending quest of mine. Career Day is when you normally see it, but I'm not great at constraining myself to one day.

A student in my third grade class in California had a dad with a very interesting job. He was a special effects artist for the movies. The child asked and asked and asked for a day for his dad to come talk to the class. I found some time to put aside and sent a note for him to come in. At the least it would be interesting. I was not expecting what I got. I love that.

All I'd asked this parent to do was talk about creativity in his job. Creativity is an important thing to me. One of the Big Fears out there in the education community is this focus on standardized testing will drain the imagination from our children as we train them to be Fact Regurgitation Machines. I agree that testing is overdone and wildly overestimated in value, but there isn't a whole lot I can do about the pendulum swinging towards that particular assessment right now. What I can do is fight the Imagination Loss battle on my terms, like bringing in guest speakers from various and varied backgrounds.

This dad had worked on a ton of the big movies out at the time. We were living in Southern California, 90 minutes from

Hollywood, so it makes sense that FX artists would be commuting from our little town to Hollyweird. He brought in the coolest stuff. Models of all shapes and sizes, things that the students could hold and manipulate and play with. He talked about the kind of schooling he had to go through to be a model maker and what a big responsibility it was to be working on movie sets. In a one hour talk the kids heard about becoming an artist, motivations, model-making, CGI vs practical effects, college, movie minutia, and responsibility.

As a coup-de-gras he actually brought in one of the velociraptor heads from the first Jurassic Park which was puppeted in the film. I repeat- I had a life-sized velociraptor head in my classroom and he let me play with it! I growled at third graders via dinosaur. At that point I didn't even care if they were learning anymore. I am no more than a big kid myself and this is wicked cool covered in awesomesauce. I'll never forget that lesson. I'll also never be able to recreate it. It was a one shot deal. Unless another FX artist's kid ends up in my room.

In Hawaii one of my parents was a clown. Not a life of the party and haha isn't he funny clown. I'm talking big shoes, red nose, suspenders, wig, make-up, don't smell his flower clown. Professional Clown. Occupation:Foole. That's his profession. Truth be told I missed my opportunity with him. I never asked him to speak to the class about his job and how he became a clown. It would have been terribly interesting. Is clown college a real thing? Penn Jillette talks about it, so it must be. Does Hawaii have a campus? How does one become a clown and what is that job like? Does it pay better than teaching? I bet my kids would have come up with some doozy questions.

On his own and without my asking he made himself a part of the class and taught my kids a little something about creativity too. Every major holiday he would make balloon shapes for each student. On Halloween we each got a jack-o-lantern. On Christmas everyone got a little tree. At the end of the year his daughter was in my room he made me a giant balloon motorcycle. How did I not have this guy teach my students to make a balloon animal? How did I miss that chance? I deserve a shock handshake and seltzer water to the face for that.

The best speaker I've ever invited into my classroom was the one you would least expect to come to a school and talk intelligently to children.

It was my tattoo artist.

I went to Jojo for a big shark tattoo on my ribs. For those of you interested in getting a tattoo, do it, they are great. Find a good artist. Get art, not a sticker. Stay away from the wall flash. Have a good idea. Trust him or her to do right by you. You get what you pay for. And don't do it on your ribs because holy mother of ink and fire does that hurt. While he was hurting me we talked. I told him I was a teacher and he mentioned that his daughter was in third grade and he would occasionally go into her classroom and do an art lesson. Up perk my ears. In between gasps of pain and gritting of teeth (seriously, there is no easy spot on the ribs, it's allllll hurt) I got details out of him. He loved talking to the kids and he had a spiel that he did with them all worked out.

I've never been one to pass by an opportunity so I leapt right in and asked the guy digging a needle into my right side if he would be willing to come speak to my class the same way. He could tell me the day and time, I'd make it work. I only ask that he talk about how he uses creativity in his work. He didn't even have to think about it and said yes on the spot. Tattoo artists are good people. I've had suit-and-tie professionals hem and haw for longer than it took Jojo to color my fish. He finished arting me up, creating a beautiful shark in the process, we exchanged phone numbers, and set a date.

I maybe should have warned the office lady he was

coming. Where's the fun in that? Did I secretly love the idea of my principal seeing a dude with stretched earlobes, full sleeves of ink to his knuckles, and an especially complicated and well-done neck piece walking into my classroom? I might have. Then again, maybe I forgot to mention it to him. Could happen.

You know how straight arrow adults react to heavily tattooed people? Pearl clutching, "Oh my goodness, how can you find a job," and comments of that nature? Children don't do that. They also aren't scared or shocked. I have two visible tattoos, one on my forearm of Chinese finger waves behind a shark tooth and one on my wrist of a silverfern, the national plant of New Zealand. Ask me about them some time, won't you? My students could not care less about them. The first time I roll up my sleeves and they catch sight of the tooth and wave the conversation almost always goes, "Hey, Mr. Robertson's got a tattoo!"

"Yes, I do."

"It's like a triangle and some blue...are those waves?"

"Yeah, shark tooth and waves. Anyway, back to page-"

"My uncle has tattoos all up his arms onto his chest. How come you only got the one?"

They don't care. Ink is part of the culture now. We are heading quickly towards an entire generation of old people who can't remember what that thing on their shoulder used to be but it looks like maybe a dog or their sister or a unicorn.

Still, a guy with more ink in his skin than is in our textbook walks into the room and he causes a stir. My class is well trained and they had been warned we were having a speaker, so they kept it together. Jojo then went into the best art lesson I've ever seen. He was comfortable and smooth in front of the class, fielding every question but one with ease. The one he hesitated on? "Did you tattoo Mr. Robertson?" He gave me a look that said *Do they know how many tattoos you have? Have they seen it?* They didn't and hadn't, but I told him to be honest so he said that yes, he had given me a tattoo. End of that discussion thread. Moving on.

After talking about his history in art and how he got to where he was Jojo dove into an art lesson. I hadn't asked him to do an art lesson, but he'd volunteered when we were talking about what he could do and I don't say no to ideas like that. I wanted to know what he was going to do as much as the kids did. Could I steal it?

He played a game called Squiggle with them, and yes I did appropriate it because it's great. To play Squiggle he had one child come up to his big drawing pad, which he brought from home rather than use the whiteboard, and with a Sharpie make a quick squiggle across it, a randomly curling line. Then he told the class to look at the squiggle until they saw a picture in it. He even turned it over and around to get different perspectives. Here's where his natural ability to teach shone through. The students call out easy things. A snake! A worm! An eel! "No no no," he said, "I see a pirate ship."

I swear, every single head in the room including mine did the Quizzical Dog Head Tilt. A pirate ship? Where? Like a magic trick he made it appear. Part of the squiggle was the mast and sail, part was a porthole. Around it he drew cannons and water, the other mast and a steering wheel and everything else you think of when you picture a cartoon pirate ship. He blew their little minds. I could see whole new worlds opening up for them. He probably had the class do half a dozen squiggles during the lesson and they were quickly all about seeing creative, interesting things in the strangest shapes. It was almost a competition of who could see something cool. It was great. The tattoo artist came into my classroom of third graders and turned their world upside down. I'll never forget that lesson. I still use it today.

You never know what guest is going to take your

168

classroom and elevate it to another level of learning environment. Speakers aren't risks, they're investments. How cool is that?

Doug Robertson

Chapter 24: Peanut Butter and Jelly Sandwiches

I don't like peanut butter and jelly sandwiches. I don't like them not because I'm a bad American, as my wife claims, but because jelly is gross. The texture is squishy, it's too wobbly, I don't like it. I will not eat it with a knife, and I will not eat it with my wife, I will not eat it in the grass, but I have to eat it for my class.

That's right, I give an assignment every year where I have to eat a peanut butter and jelly sandwich. It is one of my favorite assignments of the year. I've been doing this assignment for so long I no longer have any idea where it came from. So if I stole it, thanks. And if this is the first you're hearing of it, you steal it.

At some point during the year you will encounter a situation in class that tells you your students are not following directions well. Maybe you'll take a test and nearly everyone will miss a question because they didn't read carefully enough. Often teachers will try to circumvent that by giving the class Direction Following Activities like that worksheet that starts out with "Step One- Read all of this before doing anything else," and then makes them do complex math problems and shout things out loud until they get to the last step, which reads, "Now that you've read all the steps, only do Step Two and Three." The kids have done all this work for nothing and it makes the point that they should have read more carefully. That is a great worksheet, I love it. I think it proves the point we are trying to make beautifully.

The peanut butter and jelly sandwich assignment is an excellent companion piece, reminder, or replacement. If you are giving the worksheet I would do this second. It's a bigger wrap-up. Maybe you're stressing about your kids following all the directions on a state test correctly. I normally remember to give the assignment when I check the standards and realize that direction following is hidden in some.

The normal Direction Following assignment has to do with writing directions to your house or how to get across the school to the cafeteria, something like that. Those are fine. But I prefer my assignments to look simple and actually be complicated. We're working on many levels here, folks. Give the students opportunities to dig deeper. Every year this assignment has worked out almost exactly as planned, which makes it easier and more fun for me the following year. Predicting student behavior in big groups makes a teacher feel smart. I'm a minor Harry Seldon.

Here is how I present the peanut butter and jelly assignment, almost word-for-word:

"Class, today you are going to help me make lunch. Actually, today you are going to help me make lunch for tomorrow. First- everyone knows what a peanut butter and jelly sandwich is, right?" At this point they all nod, but at least one smart aleck will say he has *no idea* what I could possibly mean. He's never eaten a peanut butter and jelly sandwich before. He's not sure he's ever seen one outside of a TV show. I tell him to do his best.

"Tomorrow, I am going to make a few peanut butter and jelly sandwiches. You are going to tell me how to do it. I want you to write me specific step-by-step instructions on how to make a proper peanut butter and jelly sandwich. I need to know what materials to use, materials should always be part of directions. Put your hands down, this does not have a length requirement. Make it as long or as short as you think it needs to be." I notice the eyes of several students light up. I have just given them permission to make their work short. Time to bring in the effort reminder. "Don't forget- I will be making some of these sandwiches. Just because your directions can be short does not mean they shouldn't be good.

172

This assignment is not as simple as it seems. Pretend I have never made a peanut butter and jelly sandwich before in my life. Write your directions as if I'm not very smart. Understand? Good, start."

The class will busily get to work. All of them will try because this assignment is just unusual enough to get their attention. Plus, it seems easy. Making something seem easy is a great way to get them involved. It is fun to watch them go back and forth, oh you need this, and oh you should do this. Some finish very quickly. I ask them if they are sure. I make them go back to their seats and COPS (Capitalization Organization Punctuation Spelling) their work. I ask them over and over if they are sure that their directions will help me make a good sandwich. Then I collect the finished work and make the unfinished ones homework, which I collect first thing the next day.

I can always break up the resulting directions into four categories. I label them 1, 2, 3, and 4 so it's clear to me. Ones are the worst, and the ones I will present first. Twos show the second way I'll make a sandwich that won't end up as an edible sandwich. Threes are nearly there, and they are the funny ones because of the step they all forget, and Fours are the best, the ones that will result in an actual edible sandwich. I choose the best example from each category, prepare my materials, and the next day I make my point.

The One that I choose is always very simple.

"Step 1- Get bread.

Step 2- Put peanut butter and jelly on it.

Step 3- Eat."

I stand before my class and I read the steps aloud. I never read the names. That's not cool. I do exactly what the steps say, just like I told them I would. I take out the whole loaf of bread. I balance the jars of peanut butter and jelly on the loaf. I look at the class and ask how to eat it. The class protests. "No, you didn't do it right!"

"No, I did it exactly right. I followed the directions exactly." I watch many of them begin to reread what they wrote in their heads. Oh no! What did I tell him to do?

The Two is a little better, but not much.

"Step One- Get out two slices of bread. Put them on the plate."

So far so good.

"Step Two- Put jelly on one peice of bread. Put peanut butter on the other."

Aww, too bad. I put the jar of jelly on one slice. I put the jar of peanut butter on the other. Sometimes the child will say spread, so I rub the jars on the bread first.

"Step Three- Put the jelly side and peanut butter side together."

I stack the jars, making a Jar Sandwich.

"Step Four- Enjoy!"

I look again at my class, confused. I may even try to pick it up if I'm feeling whimsical.

Now they are beginning to deconstruct the assignment in their heads and say to the person next to them. "Oh, he didn't say anything about a knife! He didn't say anything about opening the jars!" They are solving the problems with the directions on their own.

The Three is always my favorite. The class thinks they have this whole thing figured out now. The Three is the curveball that makes the entire assignment memorable.

"Step One- Open the bread bag and remove two pieces of bread.

Step Two- Place those two pieces of bread next to each other on a plate or napkin."

Easy. Good.

"Step Three- Get out a knife or spoon."

This is new and good. The introduction of an utensil. But

here is where it all goes horribly wrong.

"Step Four- Open the jar of peanut butter and jar of jelly.

" Step Five- Scoop out the peanut butter and smear it on one of the pieces of bread."

Do you see what they did wrong there? Did you catch it? Because right now the kid that wrote it is sitting confidently. She might have a little grin on her face. I read Step Five out loud again.

I think for a moment.

I put the knife down.

I plunge my hand into the jar of peanut butter.

I scoop out a big handful of the stuff, and I spread it on the bread. I ignore the class' reaction. You have to. They are going to be freaking out. Their teacher just reached into a jar of peanut butter *with his hand*. They know what is coming next, but they can't believe it.

"Step Six- Repeat Step Five with the jelly, smearing it onto the other slice of bread."

I don't even look up at them at this point. It is too sweet. It's too wonderful. The anticipation. I plunge the same hand, which I wiped off as best I could, into the jelly. Ick. It feels so weird. I scoop out a big handful. I smear it on the other slice of bread.

"Step Seven- Place the jelly side bread against the peanut butter side bread. Eat."

I hold up the mangled sandwich in my sticky brown and red hand and ask if any of them would eat this. One kid says he would. The girl behind him gives him the best look you've seen all day.

Sandwich Four does everything right. They remember to use the knife to get the peanut butter and jelly out. They are hyper-specific about how you place the bread together. You might have to wipe off the blade, sometimes it's a spoon, between dunkings. You get an excellent sandwich.

From here I have a class discussion about how they could have done better. We talk about why this assignment is important and how it translates into their regular life and their future lives. Then we write Perfect Sandwich Directions as a whole class, fixing whatever small problems the Four might still have had.

I guarantee that if you give this assignment to your children you will be able to divide up the results into the four categories I describe. I want to be clear, I am not expecting my students to fail nor am I laughing at their attempts. I am making a point using my understanding of how students work. The instructions are just vague enough to allow for a wide range of responses, which is exactly what I need. In the end we all succeed. At the end a great set of directions is written using everyone's input. We talk about what the Ones and Twos did well. They learn some things. They enjoyed time at school, making them more willing to participate and try harder in future assignments.

And they got to see their teacher knuckles deep in a jar of jelly.

Chapter 25: Tetherball

Tetherball is the greatest playground game ever invented. Thus endeth the chapter.

No? Don't believe me?
Fine.
You're wrong, but fine. Let's dig in.
There are a lot of good playground games. Tag is fun. It's the easiest game. You don't need a ball. You barely need a field, really. You can just run about, shouting and taunting, accidentally tagging your friends harder than you meant to because they tagged you and you didn't want to be It because you're always It and why can't Matt be It he's never It this is totally unfair you guys. The variations of Tag are wonderful, with Freeze Tag leading the charge. Lazy kids love Freeze Tag. "Oh no, you got me. No, no I'm ok. Go unfreeze Beth first." There's always a kid frozen for the entire recess time. He's lying. No one tagged him. And there are the kids who freeze exactly as they were when they were touched, mid-stride, precariously balanced, about to topple over any moment. They also happen to freeze with hands outstretched for a thawing tag back. Strange how that happens. Like they are all running with their arms straight out in front of them.

I also enjoy Partner Tag. Partner Tag is when the kids all need, wait for it...a partner. They hold hands with their partner. One person gets tagged, both are frozen. Partner Tag is a great way for friends to play together. It's also a great way to start fights between friends that lead to dirty looks in class. A modified version of Partner Tag is Chain Tag. Instead of becoming It the tagged person becomes another link in a hand-holding chain of Its. This continues until there is a long snake of children all chasing the fast kid. They never think to encircle her.

Pac Man Tag is a good time if you have a basketball court. The rules are the same, but everyone has to stay on the lines. You can jump from one line to another line, but you cannot leave the line. It is Tag on Rails. And it is hysterical. Students will treat the ground like lava and will stand in front of each other like the East and West Going Zax until they are tagged. My personal favorite version of Tag is of my own creation- Kamikaze Tag. Kamikaze Tag is very simple: Everyone is It. You should see the expression that comes over a child's face when confronted with this paradox. *I'm It? But so is everyone else...whoa.* Keanu Reeves would be proud. This leads into two minutes of madness. It doesn't work for any longer than 120 seconds. Children sprinting after one another, dodging in for the tag but contorting themselves in such a way that they cannot be tagged at the same time. Do you run away from Angela? But Mark is running towards you. Sean is running in circles. What is going on?

Three Flys Up is another popular playground game, especially in schools where you have a ball-

Full Stop Ok, we have to stop for a second for a time-out. We need to have a discussion before I go on. I am a 31 year old man. I'm a professional. I'm a father. I also giggle in my head every time I have to tell a playground full of students to stop playing with their balls. Every. Single. Time. There is exactly zero ways to give that command that isn't funny to the 13 year-old that lives in your head. Hold your balls. Stop playing with your balls. Put your balls down. Your balls go in the bag. Removing the possessive "your" and replacing it with "the" only slightly helps, but you know what you're doing. Changing the word balls to a synonym doesn't work because then you're telling them to grab their equipment and get in line. This might be even more funny. So know that every time I type the word balls I giggle a little in my head. Because I'm a grown-up.

Aaaand, we're back.

Three Flys Up is another popular playground game, especially in schools where you have a ball basket (See? That's hilarious too.) but your school doesn't have the budget or space for many other games. Three Flys Up is appropriately named because most of the time this game very quickly devolves into a Lord of the Flies Only The Strong Survive scenario. The children break themselves up into two teams, group ten or fifteen yards apart, gather as many balls as they can, and kick them high into the air in the direction of the other team. Traditionally, this game is one person kicking at a group, and when one person in that group catches a ball three times they win and get to be the kicker. But when play area is scarce or numbers are large it becomes a team game with no winners, only scabbed knees and dizzy brains from bad catches.

The best part of this game is the kicking. Children do not understand trajectory. They do not yet get the basic concepts of Newton's Laws. Many of them have the coordination of a spazmatic lemur. This all means that the ball rarely goes in the intended direction. Or at the intended height. A teacher on recess duty near a Three Flys Up game needs to keep his head on a swivel in case of line drives. Be prepared for at least one child to miss a catch and have the ball boing off his face instead. You will see it coming before they do. You must not laugh at the noise the ball makes when it bounces off the unfortunate's dome. You must not laugh at the expression on their face immediately after impact. Parents- none of us have ever laughed at our students' discomfort. We swear.

Red Rover is a game no one should ever play. Ever. Don't do it. It's a miracle more adults my age aren't missing arms because of that game.

Sharks and Minnows takes a little more organization than most elementary school children can muster and needs to be taught by the grown up first. Obviously, this isn't the drown your best friend pool game, but it has similarities. Students need a field or a court, something with boundaries. One student goes to the center and is the Shark. Everyone else lines up on one edge. They are the Minnows. Their objective is to get from one end of the play area to the other without getting tagged by the Shark. The easiest way to play this game is running. That's also quickly boring. What you must do, then, is get creative with the movement requirements. No running, everyone must walk. Or dance. Or zombie. Or crab. Or skip. Then let the students call out the movement. Make them be silly. Encourage the silly. Encourage them to explore different levels and speeds. Again, this is truly fun when it's everyone trying to catch the fast kid at the end.

If you are lucky enough to be at a school with a playground then the Monkey Bars are pretty good. Mostly because it is amazing to watch children develop The Ground Is Lava rules independently. No one tells them that when you were a kid the ground was lava. Some of them might not even know what lava is. It's the stuff Mario falls into in some of the more heart-pounding levels of Mario Bros. Yes, kids still play Mario Bros. Nintendo doesn't evolve characters, it recycles them. Why lava? Is that the only terrible ground-based fear? What about man-eating plants? What about quicksand? Heck, what about snakes? Indy hates snakes.

Another thing about the monkey bars- have you tried them recently? I am a fit person, but those things are tough. Know what's harder? The rings. Most schools don't have rings, but some playgrounds do. They are murder on your hands. Adults forget how tough children are. They come back to class and their palms are pink and a little raw. You would go home looking like you slid down the rigging of a pirate ship without gloves on and then massaged an armadillo with skin issues.

After all that, though, tetherball is the best. It is the most fun to watch as a spectator. It's the only one that is one-on-one. The opportunities for comedy and injury are high. And upsets can happen.

According to facts I'm making up as I go, tetherball was

invented in ancient Macedonia over 400 years ago by villagers. They would take cabbages that had gone rotten and string them to free standing poles which were normally used to hold the cloth roofs over market stalls. Obviously, this would be done after the work day was over as a way to unwind. I realize you might think they would have used the heads of their enemies, or maybe sacrifices, and they did at first, but it only took a few broken knuckles to realize the error there. Cabbage was in high supply, durable, and soft enough not to hurt that much unless one accidentally punched the small metal ring placed through the cabbage to hold it to the string. That, and this is a direct translation from the Ancient Tetherball Texts of Macedonia, "Hurt like the dickens."

Tetherball was lost to history when ancient Macedonia fell and might have stayed that way if not for the efforts of one archeologist by the name of Dr. Roland T. Tether. He was not the first to discover the ruins of Macedonia. In fact, he was one of the last. But his tardiness did yield a reward when he discovered the preserved hand bones of Macedonian children and he was able to x-ray them, discovering an unusual fracture pattern. He put this evidence together with the petrified cabbages his team found, which had of course been ignored by previous expeditions because really, who cares about petrified cabbages? From this evidence he was able to recreate the game using a leather bladder in the place of the cabbage, a leather bladder being a much more sturdy and less destructible choice. He then taught the game to his children, who brought friends over to their home to play.

Soon the game caught on across the neighborhood and the local school marm asked Dr. Tether to install one of his devices at the schoolhouse as a way for children to develop their hand-eye coordination during break times. The rest, as they say, is tetherball history.

Tetherball as it is played today in schoolyards is very

simple. Two children stand on opposite sides of a pole inside a circle. Whoever can get the ball to wrap all the way around until it touches the pole wins. You would think that the stronger kids have the advantage here, but remember what I said about the coordination of most children. Spazmatic lemurs. The epic whiffs will blow your hair back. Just because a kid is taller doesn't mean he'll win either. That's a lot more limb for a nine year-old to try to control. Often the child without fear will triumph. Who is willing to ruin their Spring Pictures by putting their face between the ball and their challenger's victory? It is true that the taller kids should win. They should be able to put an angle on the ball that makes it impossible for the other player to reach, no matter how high they jump. This isn't always the case, however, mostly because strategy is not a child's strong suit. There are rules, like no Grabsies, no Tossies, no Blocksies. I don't know why all the rules have -sies as a suffix, but that is important. Also, and this isn't too important, tetherball is the one playground game I can always destroy my students at if I decided to play. Which I don't, because that wouldn't be fair. But I could if I wanted to.

One last thought on tetherball- Someday I will be wildly rich from sales of this book and I will use that money to be elected (read: *to appoint myself*) Grand High Emperor of All and Beyond. As Grand High Emperor of All and Beyond one of my first actions will be to create a Professional Tetherball League. I will enlist (read: *steal*) players from the NBA and they will compete in my PTL. Imagine two highly-athletic six-foot four dudes squaring off against each other in a rousing and intense best two-out-of-three match. How would that not be the lead story on ESPN and the highest rated show of the night, right behind Emperor Robertson's Emperor Hour, which will be compulsory viewing? I don't know why I scheduled those two things against each other. That wasn't very smart.

All that being said, tetherball is undeniably the best playground activity. I think I've made my point. You're welcome.

Chapter 26: Sympathy for the Weird Kid

They have names: Nerd. Dork. Spaz. Geek. Goof. Space cadet. Weirdo.

There are often ellipses in the sentences describing them: "He's...different." "He's...interesting." "She's...one of a kind." "There's...something about her."

The weird kid.

Every class has at least one. The kid that is just a little bit more unique than everyone else. His viewpoint is a few degrees off center. Their drummer makes up his own time signatures. The students can tell too, but if your class is well behaved they don't do much about it. Bullying is much more of a hot button issue in schools today than it used to be and I think teachers are better at seeing and cracking down on it for the most part. Still, you know the weird kids. They stand out.

Full disclosure, in case you couldn't tell by now- I was (am) the weird kid.

Sometimes they are the weird kid because of their parents. That happens all the time. One of my smartest students ever looked at me early in the year and said, "Ni!" I told her to get me a shrubbery. She asked for a herring. Made my week. If you don't know why that's fantastic you need to go say, "Ni," to an old woman. It was her parents' fault. They are awesome people.

This was certainly true with me. If mom or dad is super into something a little different and the child has absorbed it then they will bring it to school. I didn't know much about football, but I could have a days-long conversation about the Borg threat and why it would be awesome to have a Tribble as a pet, but only for a little while because you don't want a thousand Tribbles as pets with no Klingon ship convenient for beaming. Those seemed like normal topics to me. Still do.

Nerd-chic is in right now as Star Wars fans continue to

climb out of the woodwork and that's fine. Everyone knows who Darth Vader and Yoda are. But there is a definite difference between digging Star Wars and reading all the Expanded Universe novels. Did you know the show Deep Space Nine had a series of books? I did. I used to own the first twenty. They had a dedicated shelf to themselves on my bookcase. They had to be read in order. I wasn't into comic books, that wasn't my flavor of nerd, but I owned a phaser and a Starfleet uniform. I went to two Star Trek conventions in costume, one as a Klingon and one as a Borg. I learned Klingon for the costume. I got on the news cursing in Klingon. I was probably 10 or 11. I have the video. No, you can't see it. No one at school cared. But I didn't care that they didn't care.

That's the thing about the weird kid. They often don't know that they are the weird kid. They are looking at everyone else going, "This is awesome, why aren't you more excited? What's that? Basketball? Pfft. Boooooriiiing. Check out my model rocket." Eventually we all do figure it out. At some point every weird kid looks around and notices, really and truly, how a lot of the people in our class are looking at us.

The weird kid makes jokes they think are hilarious. Jokes that make no sense. Jokes that only work if you have all the backstory that's built up in the head of the weird kid. The weird kid has strange ideas in class. They seriously draw spaceships and know what things on the ship do what. They work in earnest and unironically on the goofiest ideas. One of the first short stories I remember writing was about the discovery of language. I thought it was great. The main characters were cavemen and the gist of the story (calling it a "story" is being kind) was that words spontaneously formed from noises. For example, I remember a line of dialogue that went, and I'm almost positive this is a direct quote, "Ugg ook grunt the ook growl have." Stuff like that, probably pages of it.

Meaningless noises with random words sprinkled in until the cavemen were suddenly speaking English. I'm positive I showed it to my teacher proudly. You know the scene in *A Christmas Story* when Ralphie turns in his essay about getting a Red Rider BB Gun for Christmas, the fantasy bit with the teacher clutching his assignment to her chest and writing, "A++++++++...++++++"? That was me. A lot. That scene kind of hurts to watch. I wrote a science fiction story once *only* to get the joke, "Dehydrated Water: Just Add...oh, nevermind." written down. I probably didn't even think of that on my own, I bet I stole it from somewhere else. But I needed to write it down. I probably showed that to the teacher too.

One time I was convinced that I could draw 100 pictures and then sell them outside my house. You know, because my street was heavy on art connoisseur foot traffic. I'd make $100 if I sold each picture for a dollar! This is brilliant! I think I even asked my teacher if I could get the class to help me draw pictures to sell. I wasn't going to share the profit, I just needed the labor. I saw nothing wrong with this request. Young capitalist!

The weird kid isn't simply enduringly strange, though. He isn't like a cute but slightly overly-inbred Chihuahua. There is often a darker weirdness in there too. Maybe because she knows somewhere inside that she is different. Not different in a special snowflake kind of way but more in a black sheep kind of way. In a, "Oh yeah...her," kind of way. Which sometimes leads to unpredictable emotional manifestations. Sometimes they stem from home issues, sometimes they are things that live in the child's head, but most weird kids have the darker edge to balance the light.

My parents divorced when I was in third or fourth grade. I don't feel like checking, it doesn't matter. All that matters is it wasn't fun. It was hard and I'm pretty sure the things that happened over the next few years informed and echoed through the rest of my life. I think that experience contributed to my weirdness in ways I'm still discovering. There wasn't abuse. It wasn't as bad as some divorces but not as easy as others. But I'd bet just about anything a lot of the frustration I felt as a child stemmed from it. I hit frustration levels very quickly, and would get angry with myself easily. I was sensitive to teasing. Over time I've built up an ego and ways to cope with those things, but I remember getting so angry I'd cry as a child. Lashing out in ways I knew were wrong. Chasing kids on bikes who had been teasing me with a hockey stick, trying to throw it in their spokes. I spent a day at school hiding in the bathroom. I'm pretty sure that once in a fight I bit the other boy. I only ever had a very small number of close friends at any one time, something that is still true today. I didn't, and honestly, still don't like a lot of my peers. That's because in them I see the kids who were mean to me way back when. I can only imagine what some teachers I know would have said about me had I been in their class.

I don't tell those stories so you'll feel sorry for me. I tell them because I think all of those things are true about most weird kids. Most weird kids react to situations in ways that are unusual. That's why they seem like the weird kid. I see those kids in my class. I see pieces of myself reflected in so many of my students. That's why I encourage the strange in my classroom. I tell my kids they are all weird, and then I tell them I like weird people better because they are more interesting. All my friends are the weird kids grown up.

The thing is, the normal kids grew up too. The kids who thought the things I was into and the stuff I was doing was strange still do as adults. Some of them became teachers too. I talked about this a little in the How You Talk About Your Students chapter, but there are teachers who do not understand their students. To listen to them you would think they've never been teased. Never been the odd man out.

Never been The Weird Kid. These teachers see the weird kid in their classroom and they talk about him in ways that make me sad, that take me back. They don't understand why he does this thing or that thing and he said this and isn't that strange and did you see him at recess what was he doing. There is no effort to understand, to empathise.

Dear reader, if you get one thing out of this book please let it be that empathizing with your students is a key to being a good teacher. It might well be The Key. You might not understand exactly what that kid is going on about, but you can appreciate they are excited about something. Don't be mean about the weird kid. You're the teacher, the last thing you should be is a bully. Even away from the child in the confines of the teachers' lounge, you can still act like a bully. Knock it off.

I had a student who was most definitely the weird kid a few years ago. Not only was he strange, but he had an unfortunate dental situation going on which caused his teeth to stick out in all directions, and that made it so he was hard to understand, especially when he got excited and started speaking quickly. He was always getting excited and speaking quickly. One day he started telling me a story about a spaceship. I think it might have been a spaceship in a video game, though it might have been a television show or a movie. Whatever it was, I got a five minute long blow-by-blow recounting of the epic battle. I understood maybe one word in five, and often that word was onomatopoeia. "Boosh!" "Doosh!" "Powpowpow." But he was excited to tell me and he'd waited until I was on recess duty to hit me with it like he's supposed to, so I listened. George Lucas probably did the same thing to his teachers.

I had a boy fascinated with dinosaurs. Teachers aren't allowed to say things like this, but this child was special to me. Even without the specific learning disabilities he had, which only exacerbated his weirdness, he would have been different. He knew everything about dinosaurs. Ev. Ery. Thing. He would draw pictures that were detailed and labeled and would want to show everyone in the room. Pictures that at first were a mess until you realized that this part is a dinosaur, and that's a comet, and that's fossils in the shape of the dinosaur from before. When he would play at recess he'd play alone, stomping around making dino-noises, living in the prehistoric jungle that grew wild in his head. He wouldn't speak up in class, he was very socially awkward, so we would celebrate every step in that direction. One day he asked me if he could make a Jeopardy-style game about dinosaurs for the class. YES! Then I saw the questions. Next level, dear reader, does not describe these questions. College students would have had to use Google. We worked together to lower them down closer to a fourth grade level and I let him go at it. His expression when we were lowering the questions was great. He honestly looked like, "What do you mean? This is soooooo easy now. Come on." I think about him a lot. His wonderful aides and I did a lot of work with him, and I hope he finds more teachers who understand what is going on in his head and let him explore it. He was smart on a level that was hard to see from the surface because of the depth of his weirdness. I had to dig to find it.

We all have students that act up and act oddly. They eat the eraser and grind on the pencil. They talk about stuff you've never heard of. They reference old movies you didn't see until last year. They latch on to different ideas and put interesting spins on old ideas.

Treasure the weird kid. Weird kids become artists and engineers and actors. Weird kids become thinkers. Weird kids change the world. Jean Luc Picard was probably a normal, easy student. But James T. Kirk beat the Kobayashi Maru. Calvin without Hobbes is just some child.

I love my weird kids. They often make my job harder. A classroom full of normal students would be an easy room to teach. But it would also be a terribly boring year. Sid is more interesting than Andy. Harder, but more interesting.

Reach for empathy. Appreciate how a child is different, even when they act out. They might challenge what your idea of proper behavior is. That's their job as children. Your job as a teacher is to learn from that. Don't judge the weird kid. Judging them puts them in a box from which they won't escape as long as they are in your room. Talk to them about social norms, help them understand themselves and those around them, but let them be free. Be empathetic to the weird kid, especially the ones you don't understand. They need it the most.

Everyone is a weird kid to someone.

Doug Robertson

Chapter 27: Messing with Kindergarteners

I want to preface this chapter with a reminder that what I do at school is all in fun. I've never bullied or hurt a child's feelings intentionally. Everyone unintentionally hurts kids' feelings, that is life. When I do accidentally hurt a child's feelings I make it very clear right away I wasn't being mean and that I'm sorry. These stories are not me being mean to kids, and the kids are always in on the joke. I know because I talk with them about it and I know enough to read their reactions. Kids play better than adults realize.

Tiny humans populate my school. Tiny humans of various levels of tininess. And it is the smallest of the small ones, to steal a phrase from *SkippyJon Jones*, who are the most fun to mess with.

You wouldn't think so. You would think kindergarteners would be the children you must be nicest to. That a person would have to treat them with kid gloves, as it were.

Side Note- What are kid gloves? Gloves used when handling children? That seems rude. Are they gloves made out of kids? Obviously not human kids, don't be ridiculous. Baby goats are called kids. I bet goat kid gloves would be quite soft. With goat kid gloves a person could work with a human kid without damaging them in any way. I'm glad we got this figured out. Anyway-

Kindergarteners are the youngest members of your school community, unless you're lucky enough to also have pre-k, who really are too small to mess with. Common knowledge states that adults must be always nicer to small children. The smaller the child, the nicer you have to be. This is the Inverse Property of Adult-to-Child Pleasantness. The Property ignores two simple facts: small children are human and small children are often much brighter than adults give them credit for.

In my class I refer to most kindergarteners as munchkins.

When I need a go-to example of poor behavior I often talk about picking on, teasing, or otherwise bothering munchkins. The key to this not being bullying is to make it so ridiculous, so out of your mind nuts, that the children know I am playing around. Think about the Trunchbull and how she gets away with things. I've read my class Matilda, it's the very first book I read them. I steal from her all the time. I tell my students about the time I dangled a munchkin by his ears until they stretched three feet. I make mention of tossing one by her pigtails for distance.The Trunchbull fits in with the character I play in my classroom. Mr. Robertson, who says he doesn't like children, especially *insert grade I'm currently teaching*. In fact the only thing worse than *grade I'm currently teaching* is kindergarteners. I will occasionally substitute sixth graders for that, but sixth graders aren't as good at taking a joke. Kindergarteners are very bright.

Some people might worry that I scare the kindergarteners, but that isn't true at all. They are too smart to be scared by me. Yes, I'm a long haired, tattooed, male with facial hair. Yes, I can effect a good, deep scowl if I need to. I can be intimidating, it's the way my face sits on my skull. But small children can read me. I scowl down at a kindergartener and they look up and say, "You just watched cartoons this morning! You're weird!" They know.

Once in a job interview a prospective principal actually said to me, "I see you've got second grade down as your second choice. Do...the smaller children have trouble coming up to you and talking to you?" A principal asked me in an interview if I scare small children! It was pretty great. It took me a moment to register the meaning of the question because that isn't something I expect in an interview, and it made me smile. I told him no, that they understood me and we got along just fine. I didn't end up working at his school, but I did get a job out of the interview, so it must have been a good answer.

I have the utmost respect for kinder teachers. They are saints who walk among mortals. I do not want to teach kindergarten because the idea of having to teach a group of children *how* to stand in a line and *how* to hold a pencil and *how* to do all those basic school things exhausts me. I don't want to teach children how to read, I want to teach them how to think about what they read. I always say, when I see a troop of munchkins in their nice straight lines with their hands behind their backs walking quietly down the hall, "Wow, they are so cute when they aren't in my classroom." And I mean it. Kindergarteners are the most adorable kids in the school. Tiny humans can't help it. They have to be adorable. It is why their parents don't ship them to Indonesia.

But when I see a nice, straight, quiet line of kindergarteners trooping politely down the hall with their hands behind their backs I only want to do one thing. I want to disrupt the line. I want to see how easily the precarious tower their teacher has built will topple. Because I'm a mean person.

It is easy. All you have to do, and I invite you to try this at your own school (don't worry, their teacher will be too nice to shout at you), is stick your tongue out at one of them. Just one. Just for a moment. Catch the eye of a tiny human and stick your tongue out. Then sit back and wait for the ripple. The child won't believe what just happened. She will give you a priceless look of disbelief. Then you must walk away. Word will spread through the class. Soon all of them will know you're that teacher who did that thing. No really, it was him. The weird teacher. Every time they pass you must make a face at them. Stick your tongue out. Cross your eyes. Puff up your cheeks.

The more straight laced among you might be thinking- well, let's be honest here, any of the more straight laced teachers who picked this book up stopped reading long ago-but if one of you did last this long you're probably thinking how truly horrible that is. How rude. I'm modeling terrible behaviors.

I'm not.

Before I know it the entire kindergarten class knows my name. Or some version of my name. Mr. Robins. Mr. Roberts. Mr. Robinson. Close enough for tiny people. Before I know it entire classes of tiny people wave at me when they pass, or stick their tongues out at me, and nearly all of them smile at me. Children, smiling at school? At the teacher who goes out of his way to tell them he doesn't like them? Which I do. I loom over them, look down, and growl, "I don't like kindergarteners. Why do you have to be so small?" I told you, I rip off the Trunchbull. If you're going to steal, steal from the best. They laugh up at me. They say, "Didn't you used to be small once?" This proves the genius of Roald Dahl. He knew what they would say. To them I reply, leaving the Trunchbull's script, "I was small once, and I didn't like myself then either." This breaks a class of five year-olds up.

I'm also planting seeds. These children will eventually be in my classroom. I've already got them liking me, willing to talk to me, interacting with me, years and years before I actually need to build a classroom relationship with them. I think teachers forget that schools are interconnected. We talk to the grade levels directly below and above about this kid and that kid, but we rarely talk to the kids themselves. I would much rather talk to the kids. I like them better than most adults anyway. I can find out more about the child from the child than from the child's teacher. Maybe I disagree with that teacher's opinion on things. I should do my own reconnaissance. Take responsibility for my learning.

I've gotten into arguments with children before. One kid, whose parents had tragically neglected his education, swore to me that Anakin Skywalker was NOT Darth Vader. I spent an entire recess trying to correct this child. Parenting fail.

Other small children argue about much simpler things in much simpler ways, which is another reason kindergarteners are great. I tell children than I am mean and I don't like them, and I act offended if they say I'm nice or funny. They think that is hilarious. There is a child at my school who will walk by me, point, and declare, "You're funny!" To which I reply, "I am not. I'm mean! And you're short!" "You're funny!" he reiterates. Repetition makes things true. "You're weird!" I retort. You can guess his response. I've walked past parents having this back-and-forth. Who knows what they thought? But he was having a good time. He was enjoying school.

There are Rules of Childhood. One of those Rules is that it is impossible to walk down stairs. Especially the last two. Those must be hopped. It is also impossible to walk up stairs. You can clomp, or skip, or jog, but if you merely walk up stairs then you are a grown-up no matter what your age.

Another Rule of Childhood, which I take full advantage of when disrupting a line of children, is the inability to resist a high-five. Like a cartoon character responding to Shave and a Haircut, children cannot resist an outreached palm. They must smack it. If there is a hand in fiving range then fived it shall be. So when I walk by a nice, straight, quiet line of children I simply stick out my hand.

Adults, there are things you should know about a child's high-five. Some are very timid, barely a tap. Some will give you what you would consider a normal five, not too hard, reasonable. And then there are the kids who believe that either a) an adult's hand is made of iron or b) they might be able to make it come clean off. These kids, and no it isn't always boys, rear waaaay back, they wind that five up. In some fighting video games the longer you hold a punch back the more power it gathers, normally visualized by light streaming towards the fist and making it glow. These children have seen those games. They are Powering Up the five. Then they try to explode it through your hand. Their goal is for your hand to have a tiny hand-shaped hole in it. Their goal is to make the grown person flinch or wince. David v Goliath. Taking on The Man in physical confrontation. When dealing with these kids, and trust me on this I have the experience, you must absorb the blow and allow it to flow through you. Let your arm be a leaf on the wind. Don't try to stop the high five, that will only hurt both of you. Let your hand come back with the impact of the five. Don't wince. No, take it like you're Andre the Giant.

Then, when the next kid gives you a tiny tap hold your entire arm like it's been broken.

I should mention one other thing- I call them munchkins because they are small people. But one must be careful. I was walking by a new class of kindergarteners, making faces, calling them munchkins, when an actual little person walked by. He was a student in the class. Holy cow, I'mgonnagetfiredIjustcalledalittlepersonamunchkin! No one, including the child had heard me though. Made a note of that class. Not going to do that again. I don't need that kind of misunderstanding. I'm not trying to be offensive or rude.

Speaking of not trying to be offensive or rude and failing, I organize my class, as I've said, into groups. At the beginning of the year I name the groups myself. By fourth quarter I let the kids name their own groups. You get way better names that way. Rock bands should let children name them. Black Lightning. Panther Tigers. The Cool Group Of Coolness. My personal favorite- Mr. Robertson Is Awesome. But to start the year I name the groups, and I randomly assign students to those groups. I haven't met the kids, haven't even gotten the chance to browse through any of their cumm folders. I don't know who shouldn't sit near whom yet, so everyone gets spread around. And, because I do try to whip some education on them at every turn, I start the year naming the groups after the continents.

So my class is organized and ready. I've got nametags on every desk, and every group is named after a continent. Slowly the children file in and find their seats. It turns out I have only one African-American child this year. Guess which group he'd randomly been placed in?

Yeah. Whoops doesn't begin to describe it.

Switched that up right away.

Doug Robertson

Chapter 28: Suck It!

I let my students work on their own quite a bit. There is only so much a child can learn from listening to a grown person talk at them, so often if you poked your head into my classroom you would find heads down and pencils scratching away at some type of deskwork.

My class regularly works in groups. I like group work. Group work forces students to learn to work together. A good teacher, which I normally am, stays on top of the groups to be sure the dreaded He Did All The Work kid doesn't do all the work and He Didn't Do Anything does some of the work. I also encourage tattling, but only for group work, and only with the hyper-responsible kids. It is not strange to hear me say, "Listen, if So-in-So isn't working you tell me right away." I will then turn to young So-in-So and say, "If Kiddo here works and you don't, she is going to tell me. Then I'm going to put her with a group that will work, and you are going to work alone. Can you work with her? You can? Excellent, I thought so. Please don't prove me wrong."

But in this case, on this day, for this assignment I was having my third graders work silently and alone. As I like to call it, "Independently, alone, by yourself, and without help from anyone else." My classroom, normally arranged in six groups of four or five desks each, was instead in nice neat rows. I hate nice neat rows. It looks too much like a *classroom*. A *strict learning environment*. Bleh, not for me.

Rows make it too hard for students to collaborate. Sure, there are supposed to be behavior benefits. It is supposed to keep them from talking and distracting each other as much. Cheating gets more difficult when you have to lean way over across the aisle to see another person's paper, which also makes it much easier to catch said cheater. Students often forget where they are and who is around when they get focused on a goal. I try to teach in such a way that I don't need rows to reinforce my behavior plan. My classroom discipline does not involve row arrangement unless it absolutely has to. I will occasionally threaten a chatty class with rows, but I haven't had to pull the trigger on that yet.

So why was my class in rows then, you ask? We were in the midst of the Hawaii State Assessment, which back then was still a paper and pencil test. One of the Testing Agreements *bum bum buuuummm* was that all student desks would be placed in rows facing the front of the room. Lame. So I had to rearrange.

Another Testing Agreement *bwa bwa bwaaaaa* was covering any and all posters which may help students on The Test. So if you're truly trying to picture my classroom for this story, you must include in your mind's eye random colors of butcher paper strips haphazardly stapled, taped, and push-pinned into the walls. This is less distracting to a child than a poster.

My class was quietly working on some assignment, we had finished The Test *daa daa pooooot* for the day, and the only sound I could hear from my desk was the scratching of pencils on paper and the occasional sneeze getting slurped back up into someone's head. When your class is like mine, which is to say often quite noisy, you become concerned when they are too quiet. I will be sitting at my desk working and suddenly realize how quiet the room is. And I will be afraid. For you see, dear reader, when an entire classroom is silent a smart teacher must express some concern. My assumption-they are plotting. I don't know what, and I don't know how, but a silent classroom means a plotting classroom. Maybe at recess they formulated a plan, and now everyone needs to be dead hushed so the signal to act is clearly heard. Had Custer been a teacher he would have seen it coming.

Or maybe I have a good class and I've taught them what

behaviors are expected. Could be that.

Nevertheless, a silent class leaves much potential for silent shenanigans. Thusly, I left my desk to wander the room, inspecting work and keeping an eye out for sneak attacks.

I was in the back of the room when I heard it. A whisper-shout. You've all heard the whisper-shout. Children don't understand how sound travels, but they do know that whispering makes your voice quieter. How quiet they aren't sure. This is why a child will crawl into your ear canal to tell you a secret and you still won't be able to hear it because they refuse to vibrate the necessary vocal cords too much in case anyone else is in there with them. Conversely, if the person you are trying to whisper at is more than thirteen inches away you must whisper-shout at them, putting as much breath behind your whisper as possible. That way they hear you, but the teacher in the back of the room does not. How could he? You're whispering.

Whisper-shouting is not uncommon in classrooms, and being able to hear them is not a special skill, though I let my students think that it is. "It's a superpower," I tell them, "which I learned in Teacher School. I can hear *anything*." They don't buy it at first, until I make them believe. Thou Shalt Catch Behaviors Early. I am extremely focused on catching little things early in the year, that way the class becomes convinced they will get caught if they try to get away with things. It's the same way elephant trainers get full-grown elephants to stay by tying them to a stick in the ground. When the elephant is a baby it is unable to pull the stick free, so as an adult it doesn't even try. Catch students pulling at the stick early in the year, by second quarter they've stopped trying so hard.

It was not the whisper-shouting, though, that got my attention. It wouldn't be a class full of third graders without some talking. It was what I heard whisper-shouted. I was sure

I was mistaken. What I heard could not possibly have been what was said. Not in my classroom. Not with these kids. Not from the direction I heard it.

My head snapped up. Teacher Vision Activated. That kid? I couldn't have heard what I thought I heard. Not from any of my kids, but especially that kid. Then I heard it again. I saw him say it. He leaned right across the aisle, right up near one of his friends, and whisper-shouted it into his friend's ear.

"Suck it!"

I sprang into action, quickly and silently walking, a teacher ninja until I was near enough to clearly hear the conversation but not near enough to interrupt it. Not yet. I needed more information before I started pulling ears and calling parents. Maybe I was mistaken.

"Suck it! Suck it hard!"

What the? Ok, that was enough. I leaned down close, trying to keep my Righteous Teacher Voice in check. Maybe there was something I didn't understand. I hope.

"Sir," I said, "What are you telling him?"

The boy child looked up at me with complete sincerity, and without a hint of malice in his face. "I'm telling him to suck it. It'll feel better if he sucks it."

That was very blunt. It isn't often a child doing something wrong comes right out with it like that. I was thrown off balance. "...what? What are you talking about?"

The child looks at me like I'm the crazy person. He decides he needs to speak slowly and clearly so I'll understand. "His hand. He's got a papercut. It'll feel better if he sucks it."

...

blink blink

"Oh. Ohhhhhh. Oh, yes, of course. Right. It will. Do you need a bandaid? No? Ok good. Uh, stop talking to each other while we're working right now. Carry on."

I walked slowly back to my desk and sat down. I tried very hard not to burst out laughing. Sometimes teaching is very hard. Sometimes the best explanation for a behavior is one you never expect. Often the student's answer is better than anything you thought of. That's why a good teacher tries to always be sure before raining down fire and brimstone. It might be a papercut.

In which case, you need to suck it.

Doug Robertson

Chapter 29: There Are No Rules and Everyone Is Faking It

I have a theory- No one really knows what they are doing. No one, from the president on down.

You know that joke people tell about waiting for someone to come to their job or their home and say, "We've been watching you and we know that you don't know how to parent/teach/whatever. You need to go now."? That joke makes everyone I know laugh because everyone I know feels the exact same way. It isn't even really a joke, it's just a form of racial memory shared by all people and that makes it funny. We laugh because it feels good to know we aren't alone.

I tell my student teacher all the time that I'm faking it, I've just been doing it for so long that it doesn't look like I'm faking it any more. I'm faking at a high level in my classroom. Until recently I'd forgotten what the beginning of faking something felt like. Then my son was born. Now I'm back to Square One of faking it, but this time with Fatherhood instead of Teacherhood.

I take things pretty well in stride most of the time. I'm flexible in life, or I try to be. I'm not always the reed that bends, mostly because I think being the reed that loudly splinters occasionally helps make a point, but I am bendable. I normally assume that something I don't understand I will understand eventually, and I can be patient about learning it. Being a triathlete and a swimmer before that taught me that not being good at something immediately does not mean I won't be good at it. It means that I'm at the beginning of a journey and as I progress I'll get better. Video games teach the same lesson in a much more blatant, but quicker to understand and metaphor-friendly way. In most modern video games the protagonist starts out weak, getting beat on by slightly less weak enemies. In a well constructed game as you progress through the levels you level up, get stronger, and learn new skills and tricks until you look back at those early enemies and laugh as you spit at them from your Level 50 perch. Most things in life might not follow such a direct progression, but they do follow a similar one.

I had forgotten what it felt like to be at the bottom of a skill tree looking up at it until my son was born. Until I looked at him and thought, "Oh man, now what? I have the basic idea of how to deal with this small human, but I have no trouble shooting skills. *I don't know what I'm doing!*" Intellectually, I know that neither does anyone else. My brain is telling me that when I was born my parents took me home, looked at me, looked at each other, and didn't know what to do next either. I, however, am not a purely intellectual person. I am a very emotional person. I have semi-regular freak-outs about my son. Not specific things, but general things. Am I a good dad? How will I know I'm a good dad? If I don't want to hang out with him all the time does that make me a bad dad? If I wish he and his mom would just go to the store so I can play video games and level up in peace for a few hours does that make me a bad dad? It seems like it's going to take forever for him to learn things, until suddenly he's past that checkpoint and on to the next one. How did I miss that? I know the answers to those things are varied, and I know that I'm doing a pretty good job right now and all the feelings I'm having are normal human emotions. Doesn't stop me from worrying. Doesn't stop me from sitting up late at night grinding on nameless, faceless stressors.

The thing is, this stress is not altogether unfamiliar. Even the panic attacks have an air of familiarity. I know this feeling. It took awhile for me to figure out why. I've never been a father before. I've never done anything this life-changing. Then it hit me. I used to come home from my first teaching job feeling like this every single day.

Oh wow. This revelation gave me a rock to cling to. On days that I'm feeling really down, the days where I'm deeply questioning myself, I try to remember that I once felt the same way about teaching. I can't imagine feeling that level of insecurity in my classroom now. I used to come home and say to my girlfriend at the time, "I don't know what I'm doing. I have no idea. The kids know it. If the principal doesn't know it he'll figure it out soon. I've got no control. I don't know what I'm teaching them. I don't know how to help the ones that are behind. I don't know how to deal with the troublemakers. There are too many in my class. I'm terrible at this. I'm making every possible mistake." I was piloting the Pity Plane and handing out peanuts while performing the in-flight movie, *Help!*. I spent the rest of that year begging other teachers for advice, visiting them during recess breaks and after school, digging for tips and tricks. I would bolt from school because I had to get to my second job, being a server at the Old Spaghetti Factory, but also because I didn't want to be there any more. Then I would feel bad because I should be staying at school grading and planning and thinking of new and exciting ways to engage the children and I don't know what I'm doing and how do you do that and I just want to go lie on the couch! That placement was hard and no fun at all.

The next year it got better. I started learning tricks, started being able to relate to the kids. I started watching the right kind of teachers and got lucky enough to be mentored by some outstanding educators. I began to realize that I had Teacher Instincts and those instincts, while not always great, were pretty good. I got better at reflective teaching, a skill they teach you in college and there it works fine, but can be overwhelmed by Wash shouting, "Oh God, oh God, we're all gonna die!" in the back of your head in the real world. It took time for me to go from being a guy who teaches to being a Teacher. A long time.

The thing that made the transition easiest was when I finally internalized the idea that Everyone Is Faking It. No one really knows what is going on. As a child you never suspect that the grown-ups in your life don't have everything wired. They must, they're grown-ups. I think the trouble with the puberty part of adolescence is you spend a lot of your time assuming that at some point you're going to figure everything out. Things are going to become clear. You will hit a certain age and a key will turn in your brain and suddenly life will make sense. I thought maybe when I graduate high school. Maybe when I graduate college. Maybe when I get my first real job.

Never happened. Never got the cheat code that illuminated Life and showed me the back doors and the ropes. Never got to peek behind the curtain. Never got the software update.

The only explanation is not that I didn't get it. It's that no one gets it. I'm not a solipsist. All you other people exist. You're walking bags of meat, water, and electricity just like I am. If I didn't get an instruction manual, if I never got the download of Important Information, then no one did. Everyone is faking it.

Say that out loud. "Everyone is faking it." Every person I've ever met, and every person you've ever met has been faking how to live their lives. We learn things and we make choices based on those things, but there are no rules.

...Ohhh, wait. Now say that.

"There are no rules."

Those two thoughts sprung a trap in my Teacher Brain than can never be unsprung. Everyone is faking it and there are no rules. This changed everything. I had that realization at around the same time I was really getting good at the basic mechanics of teaching- Various types of classroom discipline, how different instructional theories played in the classroom, what worked for me and what didn't. I was ready to start making my own choices right at the moment I was freed by my twin realizations. No one knows what they are doing and there are no rules.

I try to instill this in my student teachers. I tell them we, as teachers, are working without a net. We are alone in our classrooms. Our classrooms should be labratories. There are no hard and fast rules about How Students Learn Best. People have tried. There are theories and ideas and hints and clues and books and books and books but no one-size fits all solution. No one knows your group of students like you do. Every classroom is different. Every classroom is a random chemical mixture. You pour two parts Matt and one part Steve, half a dash of Angela and a pinch of Grayson, a smidge of Jane and a bit of Kris, slightly too much Kevin and maybe a bit too little Summer. Throw in Meghan, Mark, Andy, Sean, Jodi, Tracy, Maya, and Naomi for good measure. Then cork it and shake it up real good. What you are going to get is totally unpredictable and completely new to the world. There has never been a mixture like that.

No one knows what they are doing and there are no rules. A teacher's biggest headache comes not from the students who have been in their class all year, this is a chemical combination we know by now and have learned to handle. No, the biggest headache is when Cameron and Aurora from California move to town and get tossed into your class, completely upsetting the carefully constructed balance. A good teacher, a teacher with experience and confidence, takes those added ingredients and knows how to mix them carefully, how to make them part of the solution (get it?). This works most of the time. Hopefully. Keeping in mind there are no rules and no one knows what they are doing.

Going from being a person who teaches to being a Teacher is all about internalizing there being no rules, knowing everyone else is making it up too, and adding that to all the skills you've gained from time in the classroom. Then you must be willing to change. Willing to adapt.

I know teachers who have taught the same grade in the same classroom for a dozen years or more. Yes, doing something that long makes you very good at it. But, I would think it would also make you stale. The best teachers are constantly reinventing the way they do things. Classes from year to year are amazingly different. It is hard to overstate how varied each group of children is from one another. If I tried to teach exactly the same things in exactly the same way every year I would fail. At the best I would do ok. It would average out to average. That isn't good enough for me. I try new things all the time. And sometimes they fail *spectacularly*. I give assignments and lectures that leave my kids slackjawed and doe-eyed. Other times, though, the class is vibrating with excitement. A project touches a chord and rings true. Those times more than make up for the off notes.

I try to apply this thinking to my headspace regarding my own parenting. I'm not good at it yet. I'm still new, still worried about everything, still gaining the basic skill set needed to improvise and relax. I'm looking forward to the parenting gear shift. It can't come soon enough.

In my classroom and in yours it is best to remember that the people around you are also making everything up. That anyone who says they know exactly what they are doing when it comes to teaching is lying. The best teachers are faking it to find the best ways to teach their particular group of humans on that day. The next day they see if that still works. If not, they fake it again with new information.

The best teachers are Thomas Edison, finding a thousand ways to make a lightbulb that doesn't work. The best teachers are Jackson Pollock, throwing paint against canvas in an effort to express himself in a mess. The best teachers are Julia Child, breaking the set rules of the kitchen to recreate the way people see food and cooking. The best teachers are Joe Strummer, realizing that the rules of music are actually barriers to creativity and expression.

There are no rules. Everyone is faking it.

It's beautiful freedom.

Doug Robertson

Chapter 30: Reading Above Their Level

Elementary school-level reading can be fantastic. Roald Dahl, E.B. White, JK Rowling, Shel Silverstein, Jack Prelutsky, Maurice Sendak, and of course, the undisputed king, Dr. Seuss fill my classroom library and occupy a rarified air in my read-aloud choices. You cannot go wrong with *Matilda, Charlotte's Web, Where the Wild Things Are,* or *Harry Potter and the Whatever of Whichever* when deciding what to read next for your students. Personally, I have a hard time not reading only Roald Dahl books. There are so many wonderful stories to choose from. I want my students to hear about the Trunchbull, but I also insist they know who the strange and magical Mr. Wonka is, and on the hundred other hands and feet how many times do you get to speak with a real live Centipede? He simply wrote too many fantastic stories. Maybe I'll dedicate the entire read-aloud year to him sometime. Better still, I'll have groups read his best and give book reports about them. The only children's author I'm more obsessed with is Theodor Geisel, and that's because I believe down to my very core that Dr. Seuss is the greatest author of all time. To that end I am constantly finding reasons to open a Seuss story for my students.

These authors have written stories that range all over the reading level charts, from kindergarten (*Hop on Pop*) all the way to high school (any of the later Harry Potter stories) and everywhere in between. The usual wisdom is to bring a lower level book up to a higher grade, that way the students spend less time on decoding and basic understanding and more time digging into the meat of the story. I love to do this, especially, as I may have mentioned, with Seuss. Children, once given the proper modeling, can deconstruct Seuss for days. He wrote on so many levels that accessibility is not an issue. *Where the Wild Things Are* has similar opportunities for drilling down. The movie, dark as it may be, actually did a pretty good job of looking at what the subtext of that book is. It is not a movie for smaller fans of the book, but it is an interesting example of what happens when an adult director gets his hands on a children's book and treats it with respect. (That sentence was a direct attack on every single Dr. Seuss-based movie that's come out since they animated Horton in 1970. Looking at you, Opie.)

Needless to say, I and most other teachers I know love reading these stories to our classes. I love hearing other people read those stories to my class. Even when that person is a terrible reader, and you would be surprised how many adults are. There are thousands, maybe millions, of people in this world who cannot pick up a picture book and make it come alive. I think it has to do with being Too Cool or feeling silly. I've said this before, but I am in no way cool, so I refuse to be Too Cool for anything in my classroom. I must model for my students the way I want them to act, and one of the things that is very important in my room is feeling free and safe. I want them to read with expression, so when I read I always read with huge, exaggerated expression. That's what they are used to. They are used to the Trunchbull bellowing and the Whos being almost too small to hear. When someone else comes in and reads in a flat, monotone way they have trouble staying focused. Not their fault, mine. I've trained them in a certain style, and that means the people who come in need to deal with the students on the students' terms. Not that people come into the classroom to read very often. There is one day a year though.

Read Across America celebrates the birth of Dr. Seuss. It's a day that will be a national holiday when I become Grand High Master of the Universe and Beyond. Dr. Seuss is a Big Deal to me and therefore to my students. We have fun on Read Across America day. The schools that I've worked at go out of their way to invite as many outside readers from the community as possible to come in and read to different classes. They don't have to read Seuss, we let them choose a book or we hand them one and send them out into the school.

As a teacher, I forget that most adults are intimidated by small humans. Adults have forgotten how to talk to and deal with children. Grown-ups see the little ones as odd, possibly foreign in nature. Adults don't think the small things around them know the language. Which is, of course, ridiculous. Do you want to know how to talk to children? Talk to them like they are people. That's the trick. Talk to small people like they are people and you'll be fine. The one caveat to that is a lot of them don't understand sarcasm for a few years, so try not to go too heavy on the eye-rolling. The only reason to talk down to a child is that you are so much taller than they are. You shouldn't even be doing that. Crouch down and look the small person in the face. You don't want to talk to the top of a head, they don't want to talk to knees or belts.

On Read Across America day strangers come into my classroom and they nervously read from a book that has been chosen for them. That's never good, you should bring your own book. Don't you have a kid at home? Steal one of theirs. You don't have a kid at home? Go to the store and buy a book you remember from childhood. Everyone should have a few picture books lying around the house. They lighten things up. Reading a book for the very first time in front of an audience guarantees stumbles and mumbles and umms and errs and hesitations and weird syntax and awkward pauses where the punctuation doesn't...call for it. Unless you're Christopher Walken or William Shatner don't do that.

I do my best to make the reader comfortable. I have them introduce themselves. My students are always polite to guests. They chat for a minute about who they are and what they do. Sometimes, if I know the book they brought isn't great, I'll replace it with one of my own. Only once have I gone out of my way to amuse myself with a Read Across America reader. Only once did the devil who lives on my shoulder get the best of me when it came to a guest in my classroom.

One year, a uniformed police officer came to my room to read. I, of course, have the proper amount of fear and respect for police officers, as any thinking person should have for anyone who carries a gun and is legally allowed to use it. I'm not saying all cops deserve fear. I'm only saying that the way some people feel about teachers, I might feel about the police. An adult should have a healthy disrespect for people in positions of authority. It keeps us, the public, on our toes and aware. Yes, even teachers. Just because I have a credential doesn't mean you should respect and listen to me without question. You should respect and listen to me because of what I do with my credential. Trust me, but watch me.

So the devil on my shoulder decided we should have a little fun with the officer. A tiny bit of fun. I chose the book the officer was to read. And I chose *Fox in Socks* by the good Doctor.

Teehee.

Hopefully all of you are familiar with the book. If not you should be. It is an extended series of tongue twisters that get progressively more difficult, and Seuss has written them in such a way that it pulls you by the nose, forcing you to read faster and faster as if trying to keep up with the words as they dance around your mouth. By the time you discover what a tweedle beetle bottle paddle battle is your lips want to take the rest of the day off. I think it is a whole lot of fun to read aloud, but that's because I'm good at it. I've read the book countless times. Laying eyes on it for the first time and having to read it in front of a room full of third graders? I imagine that might feel something like waiting for an officer to slowly walk back to his cruiser and play on his computer while pretending to look over your driving history.

Reading at or just below the level of your class is traditional. It's a good idea and it provides multiple lesson and discussion opportunities. Everyone does it. What everyone doesn't do is read well above their students' level . Why would you confuse them like that?

Because they can learn from it.

I do it on a semi-regular basis. I very much enjoy reading higher-level texts to my students and then discussing them. The kids enjoy it too. There's a very simple reason they enjoy it- it makes them feel smart. Mr. Robertson is reading us stuff he says we probably won't see again until high school. That's awesome.

I don't bring in boring, dry things. I don't read from academic texts. I have two go-to authors that I read to my class every year.

On Halloween I read Poe's dark and moody poem, *The Raven*. I turn off all the lights, I shut the doors, and I intone by the light of my projector's camera. I tell them before I start that they probably won't understand most of the words, but they will understand the *feeling* of the words. Even if they don't know directly what Mr. Poe is saying, they can have an idea if they pay attention. I really get into it. I shout at that raven to take thy beak from out my heart. I am the raven, sitting impassively upon the bust of Pallas above the chamber door, quoting that famous single word. Done right it scares the daylights out of some of the kids. They have no idea what a bust is, who Lenore could be, or what the heck the, "night's Plutonian shore," might mean, but they know powerfully frightening imagery when they hear it. Poe is a master of tone and *The Raven* in the dark is properly scary.

When it is over I let them tell me about it. We guess at what Poe was talking about. I help my fourth graders de-construct Edgar Allen Poe's most famous work. I lead them through it. I explain a lot of the imagery and vocabulary, but they talk about it. They save it somewhere in their brains. At the end I tell them they probably will forget most of what we talked about, but someday in high school they will see this poem again, and when they do things will echo back about it. I make Poe less intimidating. I introduce them to a whole new world of storytelling they had no idea existed.

The other classic I read to my students is Shakespeare. Not an entire play, I know that's a ridiculous idea. I read sections, scenes, monologues. I read them things they already are familiar with because, let's face it, Shakespeare wrote all the stories that everything else is based on. Shakespeare created themes and utilized existing themes more famously than any other author. There are echoes of Shakespeare throughout literature and movies, up to and including children's stories. You'd be surprised what children know. They know who Romeo and Juliet are, or at least they know those names. They love stories about adventure, double-crosses, love, and revenge. They love Shakespeare, they just don't know it yet.

I don't just decide one day to read them the works of Shakespeare. Everything I do in my classroom needs a reason. At some point every year the standards say we have to talk about plays. There are a few kid-friendly plays in the reading book. We read those and the students always enjoy them. Most students are hams, and reading a play gives them license to really get into the words. After we do that we'll talk about more famous plays. A few students will have been to the theater with their parents. They will have seen *The Lion King* when it came through town or something. I'll go on and on for a few minutes about how I love plays and I love theater and they are so much better than movies and blah blah blah we get it already. I have them try to name playwrights. They can only name one- William Shakespeare. Of course that's the only one they know. How many can you name? I give brief synopses of a few of my favorite plays of his, leaving out the inappropriate parts, of course. Then I read/perform the fun bits. Part of the balcony scene from *Romeo and Juliet*. "But soft, what light through yonder window breaks." Marc Antony's "Friends, Romans, countrymen," eulogy from *Julius Caesar* (Theater joke about that play- What do Shakespeare scholars call *Julius Caesar*? *Juliuzzzzz*. Seriously, it's a boring play and I don't know why we introduce it in high school. We should do *Othello* first. So much better.). I'll read part of Hamlet's "Alas, poor Yorick." It gives me an excuse to hold the fake skull that's been watching us the whole year. We have the cliched talk about why didn't William write in English except he was writing in English. That happens. Every year.

When I do this lesson I work from my own book. I have a big, heavy, leather-bound tome with all of Shakespeare's plays and sonnets in it. When I walk around school with it children ask me why I've brought the bible to school. I let them look at how the words are written, how they are placed on the page, what the shape of a play is. People forget that everything about reading a script is different from reading a novel. So much more has to happen inside the head of the reader. It is a completely new type of reading comprehension. I let them see all that. The form of a play is art in and of itself.

At the end of the lesson I tell them they will someday get to Shakespeare for real in school. He will be intimidating. He will be hard. He might not be all that interesting ("So let it be with Caezzzzzzzzzz"). "But he gets better," I promise. The more you read and the more you try the more you will be amazed and drawn in by his stories and his use of language. I tell them there is a poetry in his words. I ask them to please remember this lesson somewhere in their brains, to remember how much right now they appreciate what he's saying to them. I explain to them that they were able to figure it out as fourth graders. When they get it again in high school it will be even easier to understand. Appreciating Shakespeare, like anything else, is not about how smart you are. I remind them that the unwashed, illiterate masses would gather to watch his plays. They have to relax the idea that he is hard to understand and embrace the idea that with time they will understand him. Like most things in life, it isn't easy but it is worth it.

Read to your students. Read below their level, at their level, and above their level. Be a teacher and use those stories as teachable moments. Help them learn to love words. That will do more for your children than nearly anything else.

Chapter 31: Substitutes

There are few groups as controlling as teachers. We have things in our class the way we like them and woe unto the person who disturbs that balance. My papers are piled in the places I want them. My books are laid out in just that fashion because I've found over long trial and error that layout works the best for me.

It isn't just the things in the classroom that are organized and precisely laid out though. We have our kids exactly as we would like them too. When it comes to my class I know better than anyone how to talk to each child and how each child will interact with another child. I know where I can put a child, how I can discipline a child, which ones need what kind of talking to. I know who to watch out for in certain situations. I know who is spacing out because they are kind of spacey after lunch and who is really focused on not paying attention.

A good teacher is in control of all these factors. Correction- a good teacher looks like she is in control of all these factors and has her eye on most of them at any one time. That's a lot of levers to work all at once, but we know where they all are. This isn't something that happens quickly. It happens over time, with lots of experimentation thrown in. And every year the alignment changes. A good teacher feels responsible for all of these factors, the controllable and not-so-controllable. Everything is set-up just right.

Then I have to go to a training. Or I get sick, probably because one of my lovelies sneezed in my coffee when I wasn't looking. I have to leave my room to some person. Someone I might not know. A random body. Ugh.

The process of getting a substitute is easy on the surface. If you're lucky you've been teaching for a while and you know people. You've seen subs around the school. You can tell who has the class in line and who is pulling students off ceiling fans. Some subs are retired teachers, come back because sitting at home all day sucks. Come back because teachers have a gene that makes them need to correct a child's behavior and you can't do that at the mall; they ask you to leave.

You find someone you know and ask her to pretty please cover your class tomorrow because you have a thing. If you're a good teacher they will say yes without hesitation. Your class is well known in sub circles. Yes, they talk to each other too. Subs know which classes to avoid and which classes are cake walks. Subs know who shows movies all day and who is going to make them teach. Subs know what class has *those kids* in them. Subs understand that the room reflects the teacher. Teachers make close friends with substitutes and the good ones are always in high demand. Someone is always getting sick, or their kid is, or their cat is. Without substitutes the whole edifice comes crashing down.

Hopefully then, a substitute I know is free. I send out frantic texts, "Want a job for tomorrow? Please please please pretty please." I normally get a positive response. I have a good class. I always have a good class. They are polite and easy to work with. My class isn't the cleanest, but hey, less pressure on the substitute then. Occasionally I get negatives. *I already have a job. Sorry, I'm booked. I'm out of town. I'm sick too.* Damn. Now what?

Now I have to call in for a substitute. Teachers have a secret network of tubes and cables connecting us to random people in the substitute network. People who have gone through the sub training, have done all the proper paperwork, and are in the system. But I don't know these people. I don't know who will respond to my call. It's like turning on the Batsignal only to have Mike from Accounting turn up with a taser and a hockey mask. Same basic idea, but widely left of center. Not that that is what always happens. Occasionally you turn on the Batsignal and the Green Lantern shows up. Not quite as cool, but close enough for theater work.

I have a special level of sympathy for substitutes because that is how I got my start in teaching. After college I could not get hired at a school. It wasn't happening, no one was calling. Subbing paid $100/day. I did the math and realized that if I worked most days I would be able to pay rent and eat. To make ends meet and to provide myself a safety net I also took a job serving at the Old Spaghetti Factory. I'd sub all day and in the evenings bring people their pasta with red sauce. It was a busy life full of patiently waiting for people of various sizes to make up their minds.

Subbing is not an easy job. First of all, I rarely knew where I was going to be working that day until I woke up. I had a few regular teachers, but they didn't get sick nearly often enough for me to pay rent. I would turn my cell phone ringer all the way up before bed and wake up every morning to a job call. Sometimes it was a computer calling me with a job, and sometimes it was the Sub Line Lady. She was better to wake up to than a talking computer. She grew to know me. We became phone friends. She'd wake me up, I'd groggily say good morning, and then she'd lay out my work options for the day. "I have a sixth grade class, a kindergarten class, and a special ed class at the high school. Which do you want?" Sixth grade, of course. She was great. Always very nice.

This, and I suddenly feel old, was before smart phones. I had no in the car Mapquest. I'd get the call, then I would have to go online, find the school I was going to, and write down directions. I got lost a lot. Before I went to bed I'd prep everything I should need for the next day- get my lunch together, get my clothes ready (always long-sleeve button up, tie, and slacks; got to look nice in case the principal is hiring), and shave so that I could wake up, throw on my clothes, and bolt. Sometimes the call would come in at 7:00 for a 7:30 start time. Not my fault the teacher waited until the last minute to call in her illness. I'll be there as soon as I can. Keep the kiddos busy until I get there.

One of my first sub jobs, and many after, was in a middle school. I got to this class a few minutes before the bell and read the note the teacher left. It was the usual stuff about the class and the lesson plans were pretty well laid out. I was basically going to be a glorified babysitter, which often happens with unknown substitutes. Lots of worksheets, keep them busy. At the end of the note, though, was a warning about one particular student. I don't remember the exact wording, but in my memory it read something along the lines of, "Beware of X. He might well be the child of a daemon. If he looks at you for more than three seconds call the office. Do not lock eyes. Do not stand in his shadow. Do not get him wet. Do not feed him after midnight. Do not expose him to bright light." I was, frankly, terrified of this kid by the time I was done with the note. I was sure something awful and above my pay grade was about to befall me.

It was an easy day. The kid was fine. He didn't do much work, but he also didn't give me any problems. I'm not getting paid a lot, and I'd like to be called back, so I'm not going to push him. My goal for the day, my goal nearly every day as a substitute, was not so much to be a teacher as it was to be sure the room didn't burn down. Yes, in the classes I was well known and well established the teachers left me actual work to do and lessons to teach. But many days were bring a book and keep an eye on the worksheets days. Completely understandable. I don't want to write lesson plans in which an unfamiliar person has to teach my kids a new thing, because if they screw it up I've wasted a day and need to go back and do all that work again. Better to use sub days for review and practice.

Subbing taught me more about teaching than I ever learned in college. I've told my student teachers this and I would tell any new teacher the same- Sub first. Subbing is great because you get to see a wide range of classrooms. You get to see what all the grade levels are like. You might think you want to work with first graders until you spend a day in a first grade room. You might think you're going to hate sixth graders, but you take the sixth grade job because you've got to eat and if you turn down jobs they stop calling you, and it turns out sixth graders are awesome. I learned a metric ton about dealing with disruptive kids from substitute teaching. The best part about using subbing as a learning experience is you can totally and completely screw up a classroom, have an awful day, and you never have to see those kids again. Don't go back. Learn from your mistake. You don't even have to deal with the aftermath. Leave a note.

I only ever told one teacher I would not come back to her room. It was the worst day I ever had as a substitute. The class was full of crazy people. I couldn't control them. I couldn't see how the teacher could control them. We didn't get anything done. I probably sent a few kids to the office, which I tried very hard to never do. Substitutes sending too many kids to the office tells the administration and secretaries (who actually run the school) that you can't handle the job. They won't call you back. You get put on a List, but it's the wrong List. My note at the end of the day read, "I did what I could. We didn't get to everything. I don't know if you had a great class last year or if you're going to get one next year, but you deserve it after this bunch. Please don't call me again. Sorry." That was rare.

My second bout with kidney stones happened while I was substitute teaching. I was sitting in class showing some educational movie when I had to pee. There was another adult in the room for some reason so I excused myself to the bathroom. On the walk to the bathroom my lower back started killing me. It felt like someone was stabbing a tiny, flaming knife into me. I collapsed on the floor of the men's room in as much pain as I'd ever felt. So much pain that I was immediately sweaty and nauseous. I called my mom, because I'm a grown-up, and had her look up kidney stones on her computer. Remember kids, after cell phones but before smart phones. When the phone just made calls. Yep, kidney stones fit the symptoms exactly. I called the office from the bathroom and told them I had to go home. You don't leave in the middle of the day, that's a terrible thing to do to a school. I had no choice. I was not in any condition to manage a classroom. I drove myself to a nearby Taco Bell where I waited in their bathroom for my girlfriend at the time to pick me up and take me to the doctor. I don't think that school ever called me again.

Students try to mess with substitutes all the time. Especially older kids who've seen one too many TV shows and movies. They change desks like I won't notice. They are flip. They say things to try to throw you off your game. As long as you remember who is in charge and don't try to power trip on them you're fine. More than once I had some smart aleck in a middle school class raise his hand, "Mr. Robertson. Yeah, uh, this girl says you're cute." Poor girl turns bright red. Might be true, might not be, I don't care. He's being mean to a classmate and trying to mess with me. First time it happened I didn't know what to say. I don't want to get fired for a misunderstanding and I am well aware that as a male teacher I am Guilty automatically, no matter what actually happened. Eventually I would learn to turn the table on those kids. "Yeah? That means she's smart. Get back to work." Shut him down. And yes, that happened enough times that it belongs in the book. I'm sure pretty female substitutes get it even worse from puberty-mad adolescent boys whose brains aren't fully connected to their mouths.

I would tell the classes I subbed for, "Listen, we can have

an easy day or a hard day. I'm not going to make you work silently unless you make me make you. You be cool and I'll be cool. Cool?" Nine times out of ten that worked just fine. Students don't want to have a day with an angry adult shouting at them. That's why substitutes have bad days, because they challenge the kids instead of working with them.

Those experiences inform me when I write sub plans now. I try to keep the substitute busy, I give her things to do without having too high of expectations. I don't want a sub to grade the work they give. Some teachers do. I'd rather do it myself. Then I see the work. Grading is a way to see what the kids missed. The number on the page is meaningless without context. I'm going to have to look through the work anyway, I might as well skip the middleman.

Sometimes I'll have a sub show a video, but I don't like doing too much with technology because I don't want them fussing with something that might not work. Nothing is more annoying as a substitute than a note from the teacher telling you to use this piece of tech in his room, but not explaining the secret method used to activate it. You just stand there in front of the children getting more and more frustrated, eventually giving up and asking the six year old for help.

I don't demand too much organizationally from a substitute because I'm not terribly organized. I had a sub "help" me once by cleaning my desk without asking. I couldn't find anything for a week. Those piles were there for a reason. I used to sub for one wonderful teacher who remains the most organized person I've ever met. She had a box. In that box were hanging file folders labeled Monday, Tuesday, Wednesday, etc. Inside each of those hanging file folders were other folders labeled Math, Science, Language Arts, Writing, etc. The folders were color-coded. The papers inside each folder were numbered and labeled. Subbing in her class was horrifying because I lived in constant fear of putting something in the wrong place. It made the day easy, but the clean up hard. Great kids in that room.

Subbing allows you to see a whole bunch of teaching styles and classrooms, a luxury you don't appreciate until you get your own room and you realize how rarely that happens. I love to see how other teachers work. I want to see your room and watch what you do. Can I see your lesson plans? Because I'm going to steal everything I like. That's what I did as a sub. I wrote down ideas and lessons and wall hangings constantly. I ripped off so many teachers as a substitute. A person has to start somewhere.

Writing sub plans can be hard because I don't know how specific I need to be. I usually assume the substitute is not a dummy. I'll leave the plans as detailed as I feel the individual lesson demands. Sometimes I'll write, "Math book. pg. 234. #2-41. Review the concept before having them start. It's in the book, you're smart, I believe in you." That's all you need. Sometimes the lesson requires a paragraph of exposition. I try to avoid those lessons unless I trust the sub. I think about the lesson plans I liked when I was on that end of the print out. I saw plans that were pages longer than they needed to be and thin plans that required lots of creativity and guesswork on my part. I don't want to ask the children for help understanding what you wrote. Please don't make me.

One last thing about having a substitute- If you're a teacher who has many classes in one day please think of the sub a little. I know it's easy to write the same thing over and over, but man does that make for a long day. *The Wizard of Oz* was ruined for me by a middle school music teacher. I saw the first 45 minutes of that film six times in one day. Did you know that 43 minutes into *The Wizard of Oz* the movie gets interesting? Lots of Kansas in the opening. Think about your sub as a person. Don't send him to Kansas.

Chapter 32: Dinosaurs and Fields of Study

Bright kids can be just as challenging as kids who struggle. They are simply, or not so simply, challenging in different ways. You, the teacher, have to find ways to keep them busy, interested, and learning. They also pick up things on their own that you might not expect. For these students connections come out of the strangest places.

One of my first long-term substituting jobs was in a third grade class taking over for a teacher who had gone out to have her baby. I was in charge of her room from just after Christmas break until the end of the year. It was a fantastic experience because she had her class well-trained long before I got there. There's nothing like walking into a situation where the table is set as neatly as anyone could ask. It was made even better because the personalities of the students in the class were wonderfully unique. Most of the class was quick, with a few students that were almost intimidatingly clever. We're talking Cosby Show levels of precocious here, folks. Dangerously whipsmart. Fun, too.

One day we were talking about levels of animal populations in the world. The lesson was about the terms threatened, endangered, and extinct and what those words mean. I love to start giving examples and have the class give me more examples. If you're talking about extinction then the first place children are going to go is to dinosaurs. Adults too. That's what we think of when we think of something extinct.

You can't just mention dinosaurs to a group of third graders. You have to talk about dinosaurs for a few minutes. Kids love the terrible lizards and everyone has a favorite. Mine was the triceratops until I saw Jurassic Park. Then it become the velociraptor. They were awesome in that movie, and I don't care if it was wrong about their size. I am king of tangential teaching and will indulge off-track discussion if I feel it is leading somewhere interesting or isn't taking up too much time. So I let the kids discuss dinos for a few minutes. A hand raises in the back of the room. One of the next level thinkers.

"Mr. Robertson? If we cloned dinosaurs how would we know what to feed them?"

What an interesting question. Think about the thought path he must have traveled to get there. Keep in mind this is a third grader. I asked for clarification. "Well," he said professorially, "we really don't know too much about them because they are extinct. If we cloned a dinosaur and wanted to keep it alive we would have to clone their food too. Can we even clone plants?" I have no idea if we can clone plants. Probably now, but I don't know about back when he asked me and I said as much. "Yeah," he went on, "So I don't know if cloning an extinct species would be a good idea then. There's too much we don't know. They'd just die again."

That feels like next level thinking to me. I went to the teacher's lounge for lunch that day and relayed the story to the others. His second grade teacher laughed. "You think that's impressive," she said. "Last year we were talking about genetics and heredity. In simple terms, you understand. How if your mom has brown eyes and your dad has brown eyes you'll probably have brown eyes, things like that." She said he raised his hand then too.

When a teacher is talking about heredity there is always a little tap dancing because you're right on the edge of an accidental sex ed lesson. When the smart kid raises his hand you feel a gust of wind pushing you towards the drop. You have to call on him though.

She said he stood up and told the class, "I know why if your mom has brown eyes and your dad has brown eyes you'll have brown eyes. You see, your mom has an egg (at this point the teacher's heartbeat leaps to 180bpm) and your dad has a sperm (the teacher's heart has now stopped completely) and I'm not sure how they get together but they do (the teacher gasps for air, able to breathe again). And when they do they share information. And that's why you have brown eyes." Then she laughed at me again and said, "So don't ask him anything about genetics because we don't know what books he's read between then and now."

My most favorite thing that has ever been said to me was said by a student in this class. I mean it. This is one of the best things any person has ever said to me. We were talking about science and suffixes. Specifically the suffixes -ologist and -ology. I explained to the class that -ology meant "the study of." Biology means the study of life. Archeology means the study of past cultures. -Ologist means "person who studies." So a biologist is a person who studies life. An archeologist is a person who studies past cultures. A hand in the back of the room goes up. Little boy, pretty bright.

"Yes?"

"So...are you a ladyologist?"

Cut. Print. That's a wrap. Put it on business cards, book jackets, the resume, and my tombstone. No one will ever say anything to me better than that.

Doug Robertson

Chapter 33: Safe Schools

"Fear leads to anger. Anger leads to hate. Hate leads to suffering."
-Master Yoda

It makes me sick that I feel like this is something I have to address, but I think it is important. I promise not to spend much time on it. I'm as bummed out by it as you are.

School shootings are a real thing and a real fear. We have fire drills, earthquake drills, mass evacuation drills, tsunami drills (in Hawaii), and now we have LockDown Drills. School children now have to practice how they should react if a shooter comes onto campus. We lock the doors, close the windows, and hide. We hope anyone out of class at the bathroom gets to a classroom or is thinking enough to close the door. We keep our students safe. This isn't as silly as the Atomic Bomb Drills I've seen videos about back during the Cold War, get under your desk and cover your head because the faux wood will protect you from a nuclear blast; instead it is scarier because it feels more real.

To address a dumb idea that floats around the country every time a school shooting happens- I do not want to be armed. I barely have enough time to be trained on the things I should be teaching. Now someone wants to spend more time and money training proper firearm management and control, staff field trips to the shooting range, and meetings about what ammo has been approved by the school board? Or do we just get guns at the beginning of the year along with our iPads and laptops, without training because they are so user-friendly? "Teachers, if you check your boxes you'll find your class list, your temporary ID cards, a copy code, your 9mm, and box of ammo. Remember not to go over your copy count. The office has extra bullets if you need."

I do not think money and time should be spent on arming teachers and then giving us the necessary training we would

235

need to handle weapons around children. I don't want a gun in my classroom. Even locked up, that's asking for trouble. I don't want a gun in the office. I don't want a gun anywhere near my students. Google "man shot with own gun" or "child accidentally killed by gun." Those people thought they were safe. Can you possibly imagine what that headline would look like with the word "School" in it?

I like to think that if it came down to it I would do what it took to protect my students. Hearing stories about heroic teachers in places like Sandyhook and Columbine force me to think about what I would do. I'd protect my students. My children.

But I am not Rambo, and I am not going out into the school looking for the guy with the gun. That's not my job. So why would I need a gun in my room? I'm supposed to set up by the door like Bruce Willis and wait for the gunman to force it open, then I, what, blow his brains out? Unless it's another teacher trying to get in somewhere safe, then whoops, sorry about the lead poisoning.

I teach in a portable. The thought of through and throughs scare me. The only thing more terrifying than children being killed by a man on campus with a gun is children being accidentally killed by the people who are supposed to protect them. Bullets will go through my walls. If I fired at a man and missed him, but hit a portable and then a kid I don't know what I would do. This isn't a specious argument. Teachers will not be accurate at a moving target at a distance. There will be wild rounds and ricochets. There will be innocent victims, a higher body count. Maybe, in Fantasy Land, an armed teacher kills the gunman but in the shooting also hits a student. Worth it? Explain to the parents that a teacher killed their son. "But at least we got the guy, right?"

I know the people I work with. I know teachers. Very few of us are people I would trust armed. The people calling for guns in schools want to arm teachers a year from retirement. The kindly old ELL teacher who rambles at your students when she comes in and forgets that it's Thursday. Picture her strapped. When you think about arming teachers don't imagine what your favorite teacher would do, imagine the worst teacher you ever had.

Even spending money on an armed guard at the school is ridiculous. One rent-a-cop? Or do they propose spending real money on a highly-trained security guard? I know, what about this guy's friend's cousin? He's trained, he's got his own gun, and he says he'll do it for free out of the goodness of his heart. What could possibly go wrong? Don't think for a second that conversation hasn't taken place at a school somewhere in our country. We don't live in a Michael Bay movie where bullets fly straight and true and the bad guys lose and the good guys win and no one gets hurt except the people who deserve it. The people who suggest the arming of teachers have no concept of what that might mean.

Don't spend money on it. The conversation needs to stop. Instead we should be talking about helping students. The cost of arming even one school, and then the cost and time of training that staff, could go so far towards actually helping these kids. Take the money and spend it on gun legislation and mental health help centers. Try, just a little, to make it hard for people to buy automatic and semi-automatic weapons. What's the worst that could happen? Spend money on schools. The better educated we are as a whole, the better able we will be to deal with these problems.

We cannot stop all crazy people. Through education and legislation we can make it difficult for crazy people to do crazy people things with lethal results. We should not be governed by fear. We should not be teaching our children to be governed by fear. Down that path lies the dark side. I don't want to be armed. I don't want to work at a forbidding building. I don't want to be governed by fear. Schools should be open and happy and safe.

Talk to your children. Talk to your friends. Reach out, make connections, help each other, find help. Schools are where we first learn how to behave in society. Teach love, not fear.

Chapter 34: The System

I've squeezed everything about The System into one chapter. It could easily be two or three but I don't want to write two or three chapters about this stuff. I want this book, like my classroom, to be a positive place, and talking about systemic issues makes me grumpy. Grumpy with suggested solutions, because I don't like to complain without options for improvement, but grumpy nonetheless. "I'm grumpy", by the way, is Mr. Robertson's Classroom Code for, "You guys really need to be good right now because I'm going to bite a head off without meaning to if you aren't."

There is a common refrain whenever teachers speak up. Someone in the public or the media pipes up with, "Well, what about the students?" As if because we are teachers the only thing we should care about is our kids. I would think by now it is abundantly obvious that I think about my kids quite a bit. Here's the thing though- I also care about my own kid. I care about my wife. I care about my profession and how it is perceived and treated by society at large. Taking away our right to be open about the problems education faces by throwing "you don't have the good of the students at heart" in our faces is dismissive, it's reductive, and it prevents the conversation from ever moving forward. We have a right to be angry, because that emotion pushes groups into action. We shouldn't fear speaking up for ourselves.

A happy teacher is a better teacher. The only way for us to get happy with the system at large is to look at it, see what needs fixing, and get our hands dirty. That action shouldn't be, but always is, coupled with faux-outrage from certain sectors that these teachers don't care about their students. Nothing is further from the truth and nothing hurts more deeply. It's only purpose is to divide teachers into I Want To Fight And Fix Things and I Want To Get My Head Down And

Work groups, and that makes us weaker. Both of those types of teachers exist, but we are being played against each other. We can't let that happen. Together we are strong.Together we can do more good.

A common complaint heard every election cycle, or any time a person is feeling particularly old and crotchety, is that, "The education system in this country is broken!" I disagree. The education system in this country is old. Old doesn't mean broken, ask your grandma. It needs to be updated. We need to retrofit it for the 21st Century. Efforts are being made in schools across the country. Fancier and fancier computer labs are going in, laptops in carts travel from classroom to classroom, and in Hawaii they are talking about putting an iPad in the hands of every student. Forget that Hawaii's teachers are the worst paid in the nation when you adjust for cost of living. Those kids need iPads! Why? The common answer is to make them 21st Century Learners. The argument that always comes next is, "Because we are training these children for jobs that don't exist yet!"

Proclamations like that have always bothered me. It sounds great and deep. It's built to shock. It also has pretty much been true since the Industrial Revolution. Today's students will hold jobs that we haven't thought of yet because we don't know what technology has in store. Factory jobs have changed and evolved and disappeared. Rosanne's tv show did an episode early in its run where she was turned down for a job because she couldn't work a computer. The ship that landed on the moon was less powerful than a calculator. My parents just barely had color television when they were in school. (They are so mad at me right now for that sentence.) Think about the leaps we've made in the last ten years. Ten years ago you didn't have the internet on your phone. Ten years ago cell phones were just getting reasonable. Ten years ago the idea of reading a book on a tablet computer lived very securely in the world of Gene Roddenberry. Right now I'd wager that you could answer any question I could possibly pose to you in five minutes, assuming you're getting a signal.

That changes everything.

The system needs to evolve to take the information flood in our pockets into account. Memorization skills as we know them are going to fall off because why remember things? That isn't the tragedy it sounds like because memorization isn't going to go away as a skill, it is going to evolve to include this new paradigm of information overload. No need to panic that, "Kids these days just don't remember things like they used to!" Critical thinking will be (should be/is trying to be) the Next Big Thing in education. In my phone doesn't just have the right answer to my question, it has *every possible* answer to my question. My new skill set doesn't involve remembering what is correct, it involves mining mountains of data for the diamonds. Searching through a traditional library is like finding a needle in a haystack. Searching through search engine results is like finding the right needle in a pile of needles. It can be as painful too.

I'm teaching, or I should be teaching, my students to look at information and think, "Does this make sense based on all the data I have?" Then they need to dig deeper, drill down, and check their work. Teachers since the beginning of time have been harping on their students to, "check your work," but only now is that so easy and yet so difficult. An essay is easier to plagiarize than it ever has been, but it's almost comical how easy it is to figure out what was stolen. I'm sure that hasn't changed, I bet teachers when I was in school could hear the encyclopedia talking through our papers. Now I can hear Wikipedia. And wiki is wrong a lot.

In my classroom I almost always give open book tests. I have no interest in seeing what my kids have memorized. In

241

real life, if you're trying to solve a problem at your job you are going to check the manual. So why shouldn't students be able to? I give them the test and I give them their books and I let them at it. In fact, I force them to use their books. Next to every single answer the child must write the page number they found their answer on. Even if she is sure that the answer is B she has to find it and prove it. Testing like this does two things. It trains the student to look for what is correct in a sea of maybes, forcing them to check their work. It also helps them succeed on the standardized tests we the tax paying public are paying for. More on those in a moment. You would think that every student in my class gets 100% every time and that isn't true. A nine year old isn't yet good at thinking critically about their work. Many students will look at a word problem that obviously is asking for subtraction and end up with an answer bigger than either of the numbers in the problem. Then they will pretend to check it and think it's fine. It's my job to help them get good at looking at their work and thinking critically about what they've written. By the end of the year everyone should be good at it. Some catch on quicker than others. We practice a lot.

The problem is the system we have hasn't caught up to the idea of knowing All the Things All the Time. Teachers who have been teaching a long time have trouble enough changing how they do what they do. Sit in on a staff meeting sometime when some poor young presenter has to come in and tell everyone about the new thing the DOE is implementing. You can hear the feet stomping. It's only a matter of time before schools across the nation give in to the smart phone revolution and I start texting students in class. It's going to happen, probably already has at some schools. That presentation is going to be miserable for the poor soul sent to tell everyone about it. Grumbles will outweigh the cheers every time. Habits are hard to break, buy-in is tough to achieve. Imagine that on a federal level. Changing the course of education in America is like changing the direction of a massive cruise ship steaming full speed ahead. You're going to hit a few icebergs before you get pointed in a new direction.

A school's most valuable asset is its youngest teachers. Old- excuse me- veteran teachers should lean on the teachers fresh out of college. They have the most up-to-date files loaded into their brains. They've seen what is coming down the pike. They have been prepared. I was in college just as Bush the Second's No Child Left Behind mess was kicking off and a lady from the government came to my school to explain the program to us. It was going ok for her until she got to the expected growth chart. You know the one I mean. The one that said by 2014 all schools will have 100% Meets in both reading and math. We laughed at her. Someone asked her to explain why they were launching the program with something so ridiculous built in and I swear on the ghosts of Socrates and Jaime Escalante she said, "We know it's broken. We'll try to fix that after it's implemented." It was at that moment I lost faith in big picture education policies. It never got fixed, just replaced. And Race To The Top is outdated and under-evolved too. I decided then I would do what I could in my classroom. I'd be a leaf on the wind when it came to government education policy. Watch how I soar.

The system isn't broken, it's massive. Massive things are extraordinarily hard to fix.

Teachers also have little faith that those doing the fixing actually understand what we need and want on the ground floor. Policy falls onto us from a long way up, and if we can't see them we assume they can't see us. The Secretary of Education does as much as he or she can with the information given, but to us in the trenches it's just another standard, just another set of marching orders and dance steps to learn until the new ones drop. Developed and endorsed by people who

243

haven't been in the classroom for years, if ever. Sold like any other product.

I enjoy thinking about my superintendent trying to teach for a week. I don't like the, "Well I'd like to see those politicians teach for a while," from angry teachers because that assumes that the teacher complaining could do the job they are ranting about. Still, thinking about the super planning lessons and dealing with sleepy children makes me warm inside.

I imagine the politicians we ride sitting in meetings saying, "I'd like to see those teachers take kickbacks and lobbyist money- I mean form public policy based on what is best for the state for a month!"

I'd hope that those who climb the ladder don't forget where they came from, but let's be honest- the best teachers never want to leave the classroom. They are making an impact where they want to. Teachers are happy to toil away with our kids. Yes, we grumble. That's probably why things don't change for the better as easily as they should. Teachers aren't willing to step up and move ahead. We're busy. No one gets into this job thinking, "Someday I'm going to run this whole state!" We get into it thinking, "This is rewarding and important. I hope I get to eat and pay rent this month."

The pendulum has swung once again towards blaming teachers for the woes of the students and the country. America is scoring low on nationally compared tests. America is scoring low on tests we've created for ourselves. Teachers must be to blame.

Except America isn't stupid. I love the movie Idiocracy but folks, it's fiction. It's a comedy. We aren't actually headed that direction. Americans are smarter than ever. We don't seem that way because the internet allows everyone a voice and often the loudest among us shouldn't be the representative thought for the group. Twitter and Facebook aren't killing comprehension, video games aren't making us violent, and television isn't making us more ADD. This is the way humans are. We simply have more information about it now. Every generation thinks the next generation will be the last. "Kids today..." You want me to stop listening to you, then start complaining about, "kids today." You're already wrong. Kids today are the same as kids when you were growing up. They respect their elders just as much as you did, only you've forgotten because you're old now. When people complain about music destroying children's morals try to remember that for a while there Elvis Presley was the devil incarnate, or at least in blue suede shoes.

The tide has turned to teacher evaluations and it has everyone panicked. Teachers are worried because we, rightfully, don't trust non-educators to build a system that is fair. We've also heard that way the anti-union lawmakers talk about us, and it's not encouraging. Non-educators are angry because they think we must have something to hide if we're fighting being evaluated so hard.

The way I see it, evaluations are coming. They are an inevitable truth that I'm not interested in fighting. I am interested in being involved in the construction of the evaluations. I want to get my hands dirty so that when I'm being judged for my teaching I know exactly what the criteria are. I welcome evaluators into my classroom. Please come. Try to judge me. But do not judge my students. You want to pretend to use a test to find out if I'm a good teacher, that's fine. Give a baseline test in the first week of school. Give another at the end of every quarter. Watch my students grow and learn. Look at them as individuals, not as data points. Judge my teaching then. I welcome someone coming in to watch me teach, but they had better be a trained teacher themselves. They should be someone I've agreed to, who has gone through a rigorous training process and they should be in my classroom often. You can't learn anything from one hour long visit. Come all the time. Invest in the evaluation. The public would be furious if I gave grades to my students after spending an hour with them and seeing one test. Don't do the same to me.

It is silly for me to insist that I be let loose to do my job totally free and unfettered. Teaching needs to be regulated. It's too important a job not to be regulated. We have many tests we ourselves have to pass to become teachers. There are many trainings we go through every year to maintain good standing in our profession. Teachers should be watched and evaluated. We are responsible for the care and training of the next generation. The government should find ways to be sure the best people are on the job. This might be an unpopular opinion but I think the only people who have to fear good, well-written, thorough teacher evaluations are bad teachers. (Before the AHA finger-pointing claiming that I'm endorsing evaluations please re-read that sentence carefully.) Maybe I'm pie in the sky and happy go lucky but I believe the good teachers will out. Assuming, always, that the evaluation is fair, realistic, and well-built and researched. None of the current ones are.

There are rumblings about tying our pay to evaluations. This is when I have trouble. Evaluations, even the ones done the way I suggest, might never be exact enough to determine who gets a bonus, who gets a raise, and who doesn't make any more money next year. That's a lot of pressure. We will see more instances of teachers cheating on standardized tests when that happens. Not because they are bad teachers, but because they have families to feed.

Evaluating teachers correctly isn't easy, and it shouldn't be. It'll be hard and expensive. But if the government is interested in doing something right, they need to think back to when they were in school and remember that most things worth doing well are difficult and you make a lot of mistakes before you get it right. I'd also prefer if the evaluations gave us, the professionals, the benefit of the doubt, but I realize that's asking a lot of some who think "educated" and "elite" are bad words.

I don't take standardized tests seriously in my classroom. Using a standardized test to evaluate student learning is like doing brain surgery with an ice cream scoop. These tests are becoming a chore, a pain, and a distraction. In Hawaii in fourth grade I gave a Reading test, a Math test, and a Science test. My students were given three opportunities to pass these tests. Those of you that can count see where this is going. I spent *nine days* in the course of the school year testing my students. A test mandated by people who also insist that children aren't in school enough. This does not include all the other assessments I have to give for myself or my school. Kids are over-tested. Remember what I said about all the information being in your pocket? These tests haven't caught up to those ideas yet, and won't because those ideas are hard to evaluate.

Standardized tests are written by companies trying to make money. That is a fact and there is no getting around it. I don't trust big companies and neither should you. The bottom line is what is important to a company. I accept that. I accept that companies exist solely to turn a profit. I don't accept that profit should be coming from my school and my students. These tests don't actually evaluate learning. Sometimes they might evaluate part-time memorization and fact-recall. That I could give the test to the same group of students three times and get three different results within a small time block says more about the way the tests are written and graded than it says about my class. I think we should do away with them. We won't, because we need to feel in control, that there needs to be some measure of the concept of learning that we can write down and study. But they are a waste of time and money. Especially because teachers know that the test we are stressing over today will be thrown out for the ~~next highest bidder~~ newer, more effective assessment in a few years.

Even grading isn't as effective as it needs to be. How many parents really know what they are looking at when they read a report card? I don't think I've ever given a student an A, B, C, D, or F. Those were passe by the time I was out of college. I've always used a standards based report card, which to me might be perfectly clear but to a parent might not be. Sure, the grade scale is explained on the report card, but the kids get not reading the directions from somewhere. Also, looking at a scale that isn't what they had might be intimidating to some parents. That isn't a crack on their intelligence. Parents might remember school as a scary, difficult place and those feelings carry over into adult life.

It is my job to be sure my students know how they are doing in class. That is why we grade every test as a whole group and I go over each answer. After we score tests and I record the grade I mark the paper with my trusty "Parent Signature Here" stamp and send it home for praise or questioning as the situation demands. It's part of my teamwork with the families. I tell my students and their parents that a report card should never be a surprise. If the child has been paying attention to their scores and the parent has been seeing the tests as they come home then all the letters and checks and comments should only serve to reinforce what they expect.

I don't even know how seriously many people, parents and teachers, take grades. Is the child moving on to the next grade? Yes? Ok, cool. Is it cynical to think that the parents who care already know what the report card is going to say and the parents that don't, don't but it doesn't matter to them? If it mattered then they would know already. The information has been there the whole quarter.

Evaluating students is hard. I use tests to determine how effective my teaching has been. Grades tell me when everyone gets it and when I need to back up and try again. In the teeth of the system, though, students must be graded and report cards must be sent home and everything goes in the files. Those files are kept all the way through school, like the Permanent Record of television myth.

Eventually, soon probably, nearly all that paperwork will be electronic. No more cumm cans, just here's your cloud file, save the report cards to it and email it off to the next teacher. Sharing grades and scores and evaluation and notes and assessments until there is so much information that the teacher is overwhelmed and stops looking. I only look at old report cards if I feel like the student might need extra help. I want to know if his last teacher saw the same thing I'm seeing. That's all, though. I don't need my opinion of the child colored by someone else. Old grades don't mean a lot to me on a normal basis.

This sometimes makes me question the value of grades as a record, especially when I'm in my fourth hour of report cards. I know there are schools out there who don't do grades and I wonder how that works. I need grades to assess myself and my students' learning. My students need grades so they can measure their own growth. Having a running record of grades allows teachers to find trends in learning, which we need to cover our backs and help students do better in school. Doing away with them completely doesn't work for me.

I don't, however, think that grades should be as emphasised as they are. I think grades, like everything else at a school, should be used as learning tools and that sometimes instead they are used as a truncheon. "You're going to get a WB (Well Below) if you keep this up!" should be, "Here's what you are doing now and here's what you have to do to exceed at this learning goal. Let's find a way to get there." Finding ways to make students care about education, care about what they are learning, and become invested in their own personal growth will justify the continued existence of grading and report cards. Those will then reflect what is already known. They are motivational tools, like anything else in the classroom.

Let's talk about pay briefly. Briefly because it's a subject beaten into the ground.

Teachers are not paid enough.

This is a fact that no right-thinking individual can deny. We are criminally underpaid. On a nationwide level teacher pay borders on insulting and lands way past demoralizing for many parts of the country. Teaching is one of the most important jobs in the world. A job which, if you believe the t-shirts and posters, makes all other jobs possible. I'm the reason citizens can read and think and vote and live prosperous lives. I should make a living wage.

No one gets into teaching for the money. We know before we even enter a program in university that the money isn't good. College professors tell teaching candidates, "You know the money isn't good, right? You need to be in this for other reasons." We're aware. I don't expect to be rich. I expect to be respected. Like it or not, the way we show respect for professions in this country is through pay.

If I can go back to my rockstar analogy, the bigger and better the band, the more their tickets cost. The Rolling Stones can charge a thousand dollars for nosebleed seats. Right now teachers in America are paid like the cover band that goes on right before closing Tuesday nights at your local dive bar. I might not be the Stones, but I'm at least classic KISS live. When you see KISS on stage you know every dollar you spent is up there with them. They earn it because KISS means it when they say, "You wanted the best, you got the best." KISS spends so much on their stage show touring practically costs them money. Teaching actually costs me money, and I don't even get pyro.

Education loses potential rock stars every day because they look at the financial landscape, they look at their student loans, they look at the cost of living, and they realize they are too smart for the room and bail. That is a problem. The simple solution is better people will come to the profession when teachers are paid better. This isn't groundbreaking stuff. It's Occam's Razor. It's simple because it's true. People will come, Ray. People will come. But first we need to build a stadium worthy of playing in. Raise taxes or take money from somewhere else. I'm not sure we need many more battleships or jet fighters. Find a way to make education important.

The system isn't broken, it's old. To fix it we need strong-minded, great teachers who are willing to step away from the safety of their classrooms and enter the political arena. As I said, teachers would much rather put their heads down and get on with it, but if we do that more and more bad policy will be dropped on us from above. Leaders need to rise. Not as lobbyists, not as public speakers, but as union leaders, governors, and Congressmen. We want change? We need to go get it. Make it happen. I understand that's simplistic and understating the problem. But it's a start.

Step up. Step forward. Get loud. Make a difference.

Doug Robertson

Chapter 35: Hello, Goodbye and Thank You

Every day of the year I begin my class the same way. My students line up outside the classroom door, I open it, and as they come in I shake every child's hand and greet them. Every student every day gets a handshake and a, "Good morning," "Hi," or, "Hello."

I do this for a few reasons. I want my students to feel welcomed to class. The day has begun and this is a good way to signal that. It only takes a few days for the Pavlovian response to kick in and they know that as they shake my hand and cross the threshold they are in School. Gears are shifting and it is now time to learn.

Shaking hands also teaches my students how to greet another person in a professional manner, a skill most people don't learn until much later in life. One of the first things we talk about in my class is the handshake. I demonstrate it with a couple of volunteers. Solid grip, good shake, look the other person in the eye. We discuss how knights used to greet each other with open hands to show they weren't armed and meant no harm. I tell them they should shake the principal's hand when they meet him. It'll leave a good impression.

I greet each child as he and she comes in because it allows me to check in with the ones I think need to be checked-in with. If someone had a rough day the day before I can stop him before he gets into the room and have a brief exchange. "We had a rough day yesterday. Today is a new day. We will have a better day today?" "Yes, Mr. Robertson." "Great. Go on in." Sometimes that little conversation is all it takes to stop a bad day.

I also verbally greet each child every day because then I am positive that I've spoken to every person in my class over the course of the school day. That might seem like a silly thing but it isn't. Some kids can make themselves very small and very quiet in the classroom. Even a good teacher occasionally loses a child in the rush of the day. I try to call on or speak to all of my students while I'm teaching. It's something I've asked my student teacher to watch me for in the past because I didn't know how good I was at it and I felt like another pair of eyes would help me be better. I want everyone to be involved in the learning. I know there are days when I don't get everyone. By shaking every hand I'm assuring myself that at least I've acknowledged every student. I've said, "You are here. I see you. I respect that you are here. I'm pleased that you are with us again today."

The end of the day is nothing so formal. Sometimes, if I'm feeling whimsical, I'll tell them to go away and not come back until the next day. "I don't want to see any of you for at least 16 hours!" On Fridays I insist, because my thing is that I never smile and therefore neither should they, that they have a miserable weekend. "Lock yourself in your room in the dark and stare at the wall! No fun! No playing! This is your homework."

This goes along with my No Smiling rule. School is a place for work, not a place for fun, and there is no smiling at work! Did you know the best way to get a child to smile at you is to tell them not to? Works every time. At the beginning of the year I tell them that I myself have never smiled and never plan to smile. Which means that every time I do crack a grin during the year, and that happens quite often, dozens of children rush to point it out. They notice that I'm enjoying being with them because I've made it something they should look for. I notice they are enjoying being at school because I've highlighted the smile as an expression I dislike.

I have a friend whom I respect very much who dismisses his class with the seemingly grammatically incorrect command of, "Do good." He explains to them that he means what he says. They should go out into the world and do good.

Like Superman. Being good is keeping out of trouble and the like. Doing good is for others. It creates a sense of civic duty. A responsibility which is constant homework. Perhaps the most important homework. I love that, and I try to remember to tell my students to do good as often as possible.

When I dismiss my students we thank each other. I stole this from a karate instructor who did a presentation at my school, and my class and I discussed why we should thank each other at the end of the school day like he thanks his karate class. We agreed that it was a good idea.

At the end of the day I say, "Thank you, class." Thank you for being in school. Thank you for your effort. Thank you for learning. Thank you for being respectful. Thank you for your attention and enthusiasm.

In return the class thanks me. "Thank you, Mr. Robertson." Thank you for teaching us. Thank you for your patience. Thank you for your energy and effort. Thank you for your dedication and time.

Thank you for reading. Thank you for your time. Thank you for your attention. Thank you for doing whatever it is that you do, be it teach, parent, lay bricks, or go to school.

Do good.

Thank you.

Class Dismissed

Doug Robertson

Thank You

Many thanks go out to everyone who helped make this book possible with your reading, editing, and encouragement.

First, my wife and son, Angela and Roland. You're the best humans. My family Mom, Dad, Skip, Summer, Kev, Bev, Jackson, Chris, Heather, and Kaitlyn. As well as my whole extended family all of whom I'm not going to name because word count.

My readers, whose advice was invaluable and who caught all the things I never saw, saving me from a lifetime of embarrassment- Jodi, Kris, Misty, Maya, Cyn, and the LaFlamme clan (who also wrote the make-me-cry forward). My photographer, Dorothy, what an awesome cover we ended up with. Please visit her website at dorothydean.com. My friends who endlessly encouraged me, especially Matt, Meg, Steve, Naomi, Amy, Sean, Andy and everyone on Facebook and Twitter who logged on to the blog and commented. And Ray, thanks for the chance to publish through y42k. It was a pleasure.

To everyone who ends up in the book in one way or another, I hope you understand and enjoy. Much love to the staffs at Antelope and Kaleiopuu, and everyone at the University of the Pacific Benerd School of Education (Go Tigers!). To everyone I ever lifeguarded with, I wouldn't be the teacher I am if it wasn't for you. Courson Way, all the way. And to every author who ever inspired me, Mr.s Asimov, Clarke, Heinlein, Adams, Klosterman, Dahl, and the greatest of them all, Seuss.

And, of course, Bethany, Matt, and all teachers future, present, and past, for whom this book was written.

Doug Robertson

About the Author

Doug Robertson has been an elementary school teacher for seven years now, teaching third grade in California before moving to Hawaii to teach third, then sixth, then third, then fourth for three years. Low man on the totem pole gets moved around a lot, but it gave him a chance to experience all kinds of teachers and students. He now resides in southern Oregon, where he moved with his wife and son, and he teaches third grade (again). For fun he trains for triathlons, rides his motorcycle, and makes small children cry at the mall. He vehemently resists the negative stereotype of teachers and fights for teacher rights as often as he can, including being deeply involved in the teacher contract fight which happened in Hawaii in 2012-2013. He advocates for his students and loves and believes in each and every one of them. He has a grand plan to become a famous teacher and infect future generations of educators and students with his philosophy, which will lead to a joyous education renaissance, flying unicorns, and rock and roll for all.

You can follow Doug on the twitters @TheWeirdTeacher and look for news, updates, and musings at hestheweirdteacher.blogspot.com. He welcomes questions and comments, so please reach out.

Made in the USA
Lexington, KY
25 November 2017